THE CHEAPEST ELECTRICITY ON EARTH

THE CHEAPEST ELECTRICITY ON EARTH

TOR HUNDLOE &
KEELEY HARTZER

Australian Scholarly

It's Gonna be a Bright (Bright) Sun-Shiny Day
Johnny Nash, 1972

First published 2018 by
Australian Scholarly Publishing Pty Ltd
7 Lt Lothian St Nth, North Melbourne, Vic 3051

Tel: 03 9329 6963 / Fax: 03 9329 5452
enquiry@scholarly.info / www.scholarly.info

ISBN 978-1-925801-45-3

Cover: The University of Queensland's very small solar farm at Gatton. Copyright of the University of Queensland

Cover design: Wayne Saunders

About the Book

While politicians and those with special interests continue to argue about climate change, and debates on solar versus coal-fired electricity generate more heat than light, a "no regrets" revolution is occurring in our suburbs.

"No regrets" because it makes economic sense to go solar regardless of climate change.

Because we cannot be assured that the next decision on electricity made by a government, whether the decision be good, bad or indifferent, will last longer than the next election, we are taking decisions out of the hands of the politicians and investing in solar-generated electricity for our homes.

Already, approximately 4.5 million Australians are getting the benefit of free electricity from solar panels installed on their roofs. They obtain all the electricity they need during the sunlit part of the day while selling excess to the local grid and purchasing from it of a night. In 2018, a set of solar panels and an inverter are able to be paid off in three short years.

Of course, it does not have to be singularly about money. For many there is also the desire to do something to reduce the amount of greenhouse gases in the atmosphere.

This "roof top revolution" is very new and has a way to run. It is driven by falling prices for solar electricity. Not only do we see the evidence on roof tops, we are also witnessing the rapid expansion of large-scale solar and wind farms. A very large battery to store electricity is now in place in South Australia. A project to increase significantly the electricity generated by the Snowy Hydro-Electricity Scheme, using pumped-storage, is very likely to be operating in the near future.

It is important to recognise that there are major challenges in integrating the various sources of electricity. Consumers are used to a seamless flow of electric power and at a reasonable cost. Integration is a challenge given that the sun shines for only half the day and the wind to turn turbines is not constant. There are solutions.

This book outlines the situation today at the start of the revolution and explores likely and possible futures. The authors have no crystal ball. However, by recognising lessons from history, they are inclined to a particular view of the future.

It is for you to interpret the information provided and the arguments made, and act in accordance with your economic and ethical preferences. Our goal is to assist those seeking answers to one of the most fundamental matters facing us early in the 21st century.

About the Authors

Tor Hundloe is an Emeritus Professor, in the Global Change Institute, University of Queensland. He is an environmental economist with a long history of research in the field of energy policies and climate change. During the 1990s, when he was the Environment Commissioner with the Industry Commission, he was one of a panel of commissioners who held public inquiries into the following energy-related topics: "Energy Generation and Distribution" (1991); "The Costs and Benefits of Reducing Greenhouse Gas Emissions" (1991); and "New and Advanced Materials" (1995).

In 2009, with mechanic Barry Luke of Karragarra Island, Southern Moreton Bay, Hundloe constructed a proto-type bio-diesel fuelled lawn mower. It proved to be too costly and heavy to operate. Like others beavering away in the alternative energy field, he recognises that not every idea is going to succeed.

Keeley Hartzer is a young researcher seeking solutions to energy poverty. She grew up in Cairns and the Atherton Tableland. Living in this area she could not but be aware of sunny days on end. Renewable electricity developments were to catch her eye. The first underground hydro-electric power station in Australia, built in the 1930s on the Barron

River, is only a short drive north of Cairns. Then there came Queensland's first wind farm, built in 2007 on Windy Hill on the Atherton Tableland.

Keeley has a degree in environmental science from Bond University, plus an Honours degree from the Environment School, Griffith University. She put her doctoral studies on hold to write this book. Keeley appeared in the *Totally Wild* television program Series 25, Episode 28, featuring the Valdora solar farm.

Acknowledgements

There are many people to thank for the help they provided in researching this book. As it is the result of a much more extensive project researching renewable energy, visits were made, and interviews undertaken in parts of Australia where not only solar electricity is generated but where wind farms and hydro-electric power stations operate. The range of people consulted was wide. We spoke with many householders, some with solar panels installed, others contemplating installing them. We thank them, we learned much.

If we single out one organisation for mention, we hope the others will excuse us. As we were writing this book the Sunshine Coast Regional Council opened its Valdora solar farm. We were delighted to be invited to the opening.

A special mention is due to the Australian Solar Council executive staff who kindly extended invitations to their conferences. We thank the Global Change Institute (GCI) and UQ Solar, University of Queensland for their contribution to the travel expenses involved in researching this book. The Director of the GCI, Ove Hoegh-Guldberg, and the then Deputy-Director, now the Director of the Centre for Policy Futures, Karen Hussey were the most encouraging colleagues.

The staff of the GCI are extremely pleasant colleagues. Caroline Pintiaux deserves a special thanks for help whenever computer problems arose. Ron Hohenhaus, as always a great help with illustrations and spreading the message, made himself available for a discussion about the life and times of Mark Twain, over a glass of wine or two, come Friday knock-off time.

We thank the anonymous reviewer who provided much welcome advice. Had we not been motivated by the pioneering, and enduring, research and advocacy of Martin Green, David Mills, Mark Diesendorf, Hugh Saddler and Alan Pears, this book might not have been written

Last but by no means last, we thank our publisher Nick Walker of Australian Scholarly Publishing. Based on his advice we turned a large and unwieldly collection of draft essays into this concise book.

Contents

Section III:
A Global Perspectives and Good Ideas

Section IV:
The Conclusion

Preface

The electric alarm clock rings. It is 6.30 in the morning. It is still dark in Brisbane. The early-morning birds are close to finishing their songs welcoming the new day. The sun has yet to do the job of illuminating the bathroom which necessitates flicking the light switch to the "on" position. Teeth cleaned, sleep washed from eyes as the shower brings life to the body and mind (a useful thought for the day emerges while showering), and next to the kitchen. Light turned on. Kettle filled, switched on, then the toaster which is fed two slices of bread. Breakfast finished, utensils, plates and cups placed in the dish-washer.

Dressed for work, and on the way. Drive to the nearest railway station and board the 8.21 am electric train. Within 15 minutes arrive at the main entrance to a 36-storey monolith sitting in a cluster of heaven-seeking chapels of commerce in the city centre. The office is on the 19th floor. A lift to it takes seconds. The whole floor is alight. Computer turned on and the day's work starts.

Throughout the day a couple glasses of chilled water from the fountain. A cup of tea from the electric kettle. Come lunch time, a container of "left-overs" from the previous evening's meal reheated it in the kitchen micro-wave, washed down with a fruit juice kept cool in the office refrigerator.

Work for the day finished and home by electric train and car. Dinner cooked on the electric stove. Lights turned on as night falls. The television has been broadcasting the evening news with little attention paid to it. It will remain on until bed time. Night time shower. In bed, reading-light on so to read a few pages of a new book. While sleeping the mobile phone is charged and the refrigerator runs throughout the night.

Mindful that we are wring about a modern, industrialised country, electricity is used 24/7. Imagine your day, at home, at work, or your weekends, without electricity. In the modern era there are very few things in life people can do without electricity. This is the 21st century after all, in the last years of electric power derived from fossil fuels.

The vast majority of us have but the vaguest idea about how electricity is produced. We are familiar with the poles and wires that bring it to our homes and work places. Some of us might not have this street-scape to remind us that it does not magically appear in our homes with an “on” switch. If we reside in a neighbourhood where the cables are placed under ground (to satisfy our idea of a perfect environment), magic is easier to imagine.

Undoubtedly, we will know that there are power stations, coal mines and at least one world-famous hydro-electricity generating scheme, in the Snowy Mountains. Anything else about electricity will be a mystery, even the wonderful, on occasion frightening, lightning displays.

The real magic is happening on our roofs. Electricity is being produced, no thunder is heard, and our bank balance benefits.

SECTION I

The Anatomy of a Roof Top Revolution

1.

Solar Electricity Arrives and Matters Become Complex

TOR HUNDLOE

> The physical electricity system is undergoing its greatest transition since Nicola Telsa and Thomas Edison clashed in the War of Currents in the 1890s.
>
> Preliminary Report of the Independent Review into Future Security of the National Electricity Market, 2016, p. 7

In the 1840s a French economist-cum-satirist composed a petition to the Chamber of Deputies (the French parliament). The petition was as if written by the manufacturers of candle-sticks, wax-lights, lamps, and generally everything connected with lighting: It read: "we are suffering from … intolerable competition … so far superior to our own for the production

> of light … at a price fabulously reduced … This rival … is no other than the sun.
>
> Quoted in Bernstein, P. (2008) *Economist on Wall Street*, pp. 164–5

This author portrayed the producers of the superseded technologies doing their utmost by lobbying the government to help them hold off the challenge. They were but yet another group of "Luddites", not workers as usually the case but in this instance manufacturers. Today, we are witness to similar circumstances as the owners of the "old" electricity technologies (coal and gas generation) come head-to-head in confrontation with householders and businesses installing solar panels capturing the sun's magical power to produce electricity. In desperation they call on governments to halt the competitive tide, Canute style.

> Australia should put the ambition to innovate green energy sources at the heart of its climate policy. This should not be about subsidising existing inefficient solar panels and wind turbines but, rather, about investing in feasible technological breakthroughs that could help solar, wind, fusion, fission, artificial biomass and other promising technologies to achieve required breakthroughs.
>
> The "Sceptical Environmentalist" Bjorn Lomborg in the *Weekend Australian*, 14–15 July 2018

Make what you will of Lomborg's statement. We are very confused, but we think he has become an advocate for solar power and the other renewables.

This is a story of the trials, tribulations, frustrations and successes involved in opening up the promise of Australia obtaining much of its electricity directly from the sun. When this does happen, we will awake to the fact that a major technical and economic revolution has occurred. We are in the very early stages of this revolution. It is but 10 years old.

The vanguard, to use an old-fashioned term, comprises a significant, and growing daily, number of Australia home-owners who already have, or are having, solar panels installed on their roofs. The details are in following chapters. In this one we present an overview—the anatomy on which "flesh and blood" will be attached in due course.

We note in passing that others are coming to recognise that something very interesting is happening in Australia. One example is found on the front cover of *New Scientist* of 9 June 2018. It reads: "100% Renewables: How to keep the lights on without blowing the planet."

Go to the feature article inside and Australia gets several mentions. The underlying theme, to quote the article, is "clean becomes cheap".

Australia's geography blesses it with brilliant sunshine somewhere in the country, if not across its whole domain, on each and any day of the year. The country's immense size, stretching east to west approximately 4,000 kilometres, and south to north about 3,500 kilometres means that when there are torrential, tropical downpours in the north, the remainder of the country can be bathed in sunlight. When the occasional blizzard blows across the Australian Alps, Darwin is blue-skies cloudless. Unfortunately, Australia's natural physical geography is not overlayed by its human geography. This we will come to see is a challenge if we are to make the most out of nature's bountiful sunshine.

Nearly all of Australians (in the order 90 per cent) live on or near to the coast; and except for Adelaide, Perth, Darwin and a few small towns this means the east coast. Where the population is, so is industry and commerce. This is where electricity is required in vast amounts. And here is the bad luck. In the vast outback, deserts bathed in sun are available to host enormous solar farms on land of little other use, but they far from major population centres and industry. The question is we can bring at a reasonable cost electricity generated in the middle of the nation to the coastal cities? If this proves possible, the renewable electricity revolution will jump to another plane. There are other possibilities just as exciting.

We recognise that Australia is constrained by the amount of sunshine available on a daily basis to provide continuous solar electricity; and that at this moment in time batteries to be used to store electricity when the sun does not shine are expensive. We are bombarded with the word "intermittency" by those who are genuinely pessimistic as to the ability of solar electricity to be but a niche product and by those who oppose it on ideological grounds. The intermittency story is about the difficulty (at present) in integrating the transmission and distribution of solar electricity, which fluctuates over a 24-hour period, with coal-generated, gas-fired and hydro-electricity, all of which can run uninterrupted throughout day and night. Wind power is in the same category as solar; it does not blow constantly at the required speed, and at times it is breathless still. Households, commercial establishments, industrial firms and farms demand seamless electricity. To succeed the solar revolution requires us to overcome intermittency. Fortunately, there are practical solutions.

First, consider the solar electricity generated when the sun is shining and not used then and there. It needs to be stored and made available for use when it is dark. We are conditioned to immediately think of batteries that will sit beside our dwellings and businesses and store the excess electricity generated by the photovoltaic panels attached to our roofs or sitting on the ground next to our buildings. The fact that few of us have these batteries means that they are costly at present. Yet, there is market place evidence that their price is falling, and battery manufacturers assert the downward price trend has a considerable way to go. Both small (household-scale) and large (factory-scale or larger) batteries are clearly in the mix for a renewable electricity future. We will return to discuss batteries in more detail as battery storage is one of a number of options.

One particular form of solar-powered electricity has the potential to deal with intermittency, at least over a short time period. There are solar farms (as opposed to individual roof-top photovoltaic panels) using the "thermal solar" process.

Using this technology, the sun's heat is gathered by a "farm" of mirrors arranged in a sunny location and then concentrated to heat various materials which store the heat until it is required to produce steam which, as with burning coal, produces electricity. The duration that the heat can be stored varies from a few hours to 24 hours. Obviously, this would be too short a period if there were extended breakdowns in electricity generation or periods with little sunlight.

Spain, the US and Morocco are countries with significant thermal solar. In the US and Morocco thermal solar sites are in deserts—good sunlight and very little rain. Desert environments bring their particular downsides, with dust being the standout one and very little precious water available for cleaning the panels or dishes. This would be a consideration if thermal solar farms were to be sited in Australian deserts.

Plans for a specific type of thermal solar farm on the Darling Downs, at Kogan Creek, were well advanced in the beginning of the 21st century. It was not to be a conventional thermal solar plant to produce electricity to be fed into a grid. Its goal was to boost the efficiency of the neighbouring coal-fired power station by producing heat. It was appropriately called "Solar Boost". The heat-gathering panels were installed at considerable cost, but the project did not proceed due to, apparently, "financial reasons", a term that covers a wide range of problems. The failure of this project, well after the "sods were turned", the traditional signal that something big is about to happen, was bad publicity for solar power. Trials and tribulations must be expected.

To another solution to the intermittency problem, there is one source of renewable electricity which is not intermittent, hydro-electricity. It is a 24 hour per day source of electricity which can be turned on or off within a minute, hence can be used as "base-load power" or "peak demand" electricity. As these terms suggest, the former relates to the regular supply throughout a normal day, while the latter is called on in morning and evening periods when much electricity is used for cooking, showers and air-conditioning.

With a major exception and two minor ones plus a fully-developed proposal, pumped-storage hydro-electricity is still in a conceptual phase in Australia. However, it is considered to have significant potential; on economic grounds it is considered to be the best form of storing renewable electricity. Other countries are looking to pumped-storage hydro-electricity as the solution to intermittency. Consider Norway as an example. Norway produces virtually 100 per cent of its electricity by conventional hydro power plants. Proposals are on drawing boards to construct pumped-storage hydro-electricity power stations in Norway to export electricity to Germany, in the latter's quest to become a totally renewable electricity nation.

The existing pumped-storage schemes in Australia are the large one as part of the Snowy Mountains hydro-electric scheme; the multi-purpose Wivenhoe dam on the Brisbane River (a very small but under-utilised pumped-storage capability); and, the Kangaroo Valley Power Station. Much potential exists in Tasmania to add pumped-storage to its hydro-electricity output. Tasmania has abundant rain and snow, controlled by dams and reservoirs—some extremely controversial and only constructed in spite of immense opposition. In a normal year, Tasmania produces all the electricity it needs and exports the surplus by an undersea link to the mainland. With heightened dam walls and reservoirs, Tasmania could export very large amounts of renewable electricity to the mainland. We note that there is likely to be opposition to constructing more reservoirs and heightening dam walls in Tasmania. There is a strong "green" lobby in the state and the benefits of renewable electricity might not outweigh "wilderness romanticism". Time will tell.

Our major hydro-electricity scheme is a world icon, the Snowy Mountains Hydro-Electricity Scheme (to give it its formal title). It produces a large amount of electricity which feeds into the grid that supplies all the Australian east coast and west to Port Lincoln in South Australia. (This grid is alternatively known as the "East Coast Grid" or the "National Electricity Transmission Grid", although both titles do not confirm to geographical reality.)

In addition, the Snowy scheme produces an enormous amount of water that irrigates the otherwise poor rainfall plains to the west, creating Australia's "food bowl". The vast bulk of the scheme's hydro-electric power is produced by falling water turning turbines. However, it does not have to be a one-way flow of water. The water that falls to turn the turbines that produce the electricity can be returned to the storage above from where it fell, to once again fall and generate electricity. This can continue indefinitely. Of course, electricity is used in pumping this water back up, but here is the beauty of the process. The electricity to do that can be drawn from a renewable resource, for example, surplus solar electricity in an off-peak period in the middle of the day.

We have one large-scale pumped-storage power station in Australia. It is the Snowy Mountains "Tumut 3" pumped-storage hydro-electric power station above the Talbingo reservoir. This is a model to solve the intermittency of sun and wind generated electricity. In Australia we have neglected this technology until recently. We have tended to think of hydro-electricity simply as derived from water that gushes over waterfalls, with a turbine at the bottom then allowing water, having done its job in producing electricity, flow into a river and "away".

The future of electricity is to be founded on a series of changes in thinking (paradigm shifts in the jargon of the experts). Pumped-storage facilities, appropriately placed along the high country that runs adjacent to our east coast cities, towns, industries and river-valley farms have the potential to solve the intermittency problem of solar and wind-generated electricity for the eastern part of the nation. A similar opportunity exists for the west of the nation, and in coastal regions with high coastal cliffs. Salt water pumped from the ocean below could be used. This is the future. It takes time for new ideas, however valuable, to be accepted and then more time for action, such as the necessary infrastructure to be built.

The very near future is going to be more and more of intermittent electricity, notwithstanding the problems it can create. A vastly increased solar and wind power capacity is building rapidly, with an increasing number of households and businesses installing photovoltaic roof panels, and a spurt of solar and wind farms being built around the country. To address intermittency, this will, if pumped-storage hydro-electricity is accepted as the solution to smoothing-out the flow of electricity to meet demand, require urgent action to commence building pumped-storage hydro-electricity schemes where needed around the nation.

We expect to see a very large-scale pumped-storage hydro-electricity project to be built in the near future, but it will not be completed over night. Up to four to six years could be required. We refer to what is being called Snowy 2.0, an extension of the Snowy Mountains scheme. Its electricity will be fed in the east coast grid and be very important in the overall flow of electricity for the eastern part of Australia, but by itself it will not be enough. We have moved ahead of the story.

As noted in our introductory remarks, much of the land suited for large-scale solar farms is in the distant outback. It is suited because it gets extensive sunlight for most of the year and it is of little economic value in other uses. We are referring to arid and semi-arid country, suitable at the best for extensive sheep and cattle grazing. In economic terms, covering this land with solar panels comes at insignificant opportunity cost. What this refers to is the fact that on a per hectare basis more profit is to be made from solar electricity than beef or wool. This is the case if the electricity is used near to the solar farms, for example in Indigenous communities and the small rural towns that exist here and there, in no uniform pattern, in the Australian outback.

Transmitting electricity from the centre of Australia to the major population and industrial centres is an entirely different matter. The cost of outback solar electricity on the east coast would be determined by the expense of building an extensive grid. The existing one goes only about half way across Queensland. It could be extended but would in any case require upgrading. In certain parts of the outback, the south-west, west, north-west and north of Australia, the arid and semi-arid lands come close to the coast, and transmission lines would not have to be as long and expensive as ones heading east from the centre. When we come to outline the proposal to export electricity to Australia's northern neighbour, the electricity would be sourced from solar farms on low value land near the Western Australian coast.

Local use of solar electricity, as is possibly in the outback, is certainly an economic and environmental benefit. With battery storage it could result in the demise of diesel generators, which are costly in fuel and make their contribution to greenhouse gas emissions. Without battery storage, small-scale solar farms can have their electricity production supplemented by diesel generators, while not the optimal case, it is an improvement on the present.

The gains from building utility-scale (meaning they have the output capacity of a conventional coal-fired power station) solar farms in the outback will come about if electricity can be transmitted to the major cities and industrial areas of the nation at a reasonable cost. The cost is a matter to be determined. As would be obvious to anyone who has crossed this vast country, very long distances are involved in travelling from, say, Alice Springs to Brisbane. Something closer to being "national" than the grid commonly called the National Electricity Market will be required. High voltage power lines and much improved interconnectors will be needed. One positive factor is that transmission losses have reduced in recent years.

It is obvious that in a cost-benefit analysis of transmitting solar-generated electricity from the centre of Australia to the coast will involve not just the cost of transporting materials and building large solar farms, the cost of maintaining the farms in a hostile, hot and of occasion dusty environment, but also include the cost of the major infrastructure to transmit the electricity to where it is needed. This project would not be a duplicate of the existing very long grid (from north Queensland into Victoria and across to South Australia) for the simple reason that the existing grid services a very large number of cities and towns plus major industries as it meanders down and along the coastal strip. There is little need for a centre-to-the-coast grid to service cities, towns or major industries as it crosses the nation. They don't exist.

We need to be realistic about the role that Australia's vast desert-like outback could play in the future of renewable electricity. There would seem to be a smidgen of outbackphilia at play. Yet, the advocates of giant solar farms in Australian deserts are many and excellent scientists. We will meet some in due course.

It does not have to be barren, relatively worthless, land in the middle of the nation where large solar farms are built. The investors in solar farms are not waiting for new grids and their sophisticated associated infrastructure to be built. They are seeking out and finding suitable sites in relative proximity to the existing grids. The closer to a grid the better the economics. However, the opportunity cost of taking this better land out of agriculture is considerably higher than targeting desert country. And as we will see, conflicts are inevitable when solar farms are located near to human settlements, or the argument can be made that good agricultural land is being covered by the panels.

Ultimately, economics will determine what is built where and when. The long term could see vast solar farms in the outback and they might provide electricity for other than the domestic market. This is explored in a future chapter. The key as always is the economics. At present both the rush of solar and wind farms are finding sites near to the existing grids, and in most cases not causing conflict with other land uses.

There are two distinct economic sums to be done in comparing renewable electricity with fossil-fuel generated electricity. One is where climate change is ignored, in other words no carbon tax is included in the price paid for electricity generated by burning coal or the other fossil fuels. All other things being equal, this favours a longer life for fossil-fuel-generated electricity. The other analysis includes an additional cost of electricity based on the damage expected to be done by global warming, for example, the damage might be a significant loss of agricultural productivity and, hence, income for farmers. A carbon tax would be set to compensate for this and any other losses and increase the price we pay for electricity.

Unresolved at present is a realistic "price of carbon". In future chapters we will need to select a carbon price so to illustrate the potential value of renewable electricity "offsets". Assuming (guessing) a carbon price is far from ideal, yet our scientists, notwithstanding very much hard work, are struggling to make fine scale predictions of climate change damages, most of which are still in the distant future. The economics of climate change is dependent on the results of climatological, agronomic and epidemiological research. Much remains uncertain at present. A few brave economists have estimated the damage cost of global warming and we will refer to their estimates later.

The points just made noted, there is no point in letting one of a number of difficult issues stymy the evaluation of a solar-energy future. The immediate focus needs to be what happens now in terms of electricity generation and transmission.

With households sending excess solar-generated electricity into the major grids, and with more and more solar and wind farms also feeding into the grids, we would expect disruption of the existing business model which, understandably, is based on a century old practice of a one-way flow of electricity—from a coal or gas power station to a consumer. Already, there are well over one-and-a-half million Australian solar-powered households putting their individual small amounts of surplus electricity into a grid. This is a completely novel situation.

Go back 10 years and there were virtually no solar powered households.

It helps in understanding the issues we will come to in future chapters if we explain certain features of the existing electricity generation, transmission and distribution system. While it has been changed by governments over the past 20 years, governments could not anticipate the success of the recent solar revolution and hence the system remains in fundamental ways incompatible with the evolving solar electricity revolution.

The first thing to note is that there was a major public inquiry in the early 1990s, undertaken by the Industry Commission. The Industry Commission had a very strong pro-market, anti-government ideological stance. It followed that its recommendations would favour "opening up" the electricity system to competition. This was no easy task where parts of the industry have inherent natural monopoly characteristics. There is no point in having two or more sets of poles and wires running down your street. Imagine the unnecessary cost. Hence monopoly.

At the time the inquiry took place, the electricity business was, in most states and territories, in the hands of governments. There were no solar panels on household roofs, or solar and wind farms; hence there was no need to consider residents selling excess electricity into a grid. There was none to sell. In 1990 and 1991, the Commission's task was relatively easy, yet, politically fraught. The then Victorian government was moving to privatise the electricity industry. This ran counter to a widely held public understanding that electricity, like water supply and a number of public services, was to be a publicly-owned part of the economy. There was a real concern that the Industry Commission would recommend privatisation of the electricity industry.

That aside, there was one issue on which the inquiry failed to deliver the results it promised. The majority view of the commissioners was that government-owned electricity business would over-spend, "gold-plate" it was called, on infrastructure such as poles and wires. The thinking was, rightly or wrongly, that this would occur because there was no competitive pressure from other firms in the same business, and lax government oversight would not control the spending by the government-owned enterprises.

To address this wasteful spending, the commissioners sought to bring to bear the pressures of competition. A gold-plated electricity transmitter and/or distributor would not be able to compete on price with a cost-conscious competitor, as one might expect a private electricity firm to be. If actual competition was not feasible, there had to be a way of getting the government owned businesses to operate in a de facto competitive framework. This is where the idea of "corporatisation" came into play.

Amongst a number of recommendations made by the commissioners, a fundamental one was that the distinct elements of the electricity business (generation, distribution and retailing of electricity) were to be separated and each part "corporatized". This was a step removed from the privatisation that some feared—actually a fundamentally different arrangement to privatisation. The concept of corporatization can be simplified to mean: act as if your part of the electricity business is a private firm attempting to return a normal dividend to its shareholders. Cut costs where possible. Set prices that delivered a market rate of return on the dollars invested in the industry. The difference between privatisation and corporatisation was ownership of the mines, poles and wires and distribution networks. Under the latter the shareholders would be ministers of the State or Territory governments. This meant the revenue from electricity sales went to our governments, and we would presumably benefit from the spending of that money. Of course, this could be and was a matter of contention.

To this very day over-spending on poles and wires, the practice of gold plating, remains a significant economic problem and is the main, if not the only, cause of higher-than-necessary electricity prices at present. The corporatized entities found reasons to upgrade their electricity delivery infrastructure. They were capable of running a case that convinced (possibly baffled) the governments overseeing them. This is not unusual where there are highly technical skills in an organisation reporting to lay people, as government ministers tend to be. Even if the relevant ministers can draw on expert advice in their departments, the fine detail which can make or break a decision is in the hands of the electricity organisations.

Today, electricity consumers in NSW, Queensland and Tasmania are paying for major expenditure on unnecessary upgrades of poles and wires. According to the Grattan Institute, in its 2018 report "Down to the Wire", electricity consumers in these states are paying anything between $100 and $400 extra per year. The less well informed are prone to blame this increase in their electricity price on those households with solar panels installed; if not them, wind farms or both. Some politicians have found it convenient to point their fingers in this direction. For these folks there is "good" electricity, it comes from burning coal, and there is "bad" electricity, it comes either directly or indirectly from the sun.

Prior to the changes that followed the Industry Commission inquiry, the business model was one of an integrated electricity supply chain of generation, transmission and distribution. Governments owned the total system, sometimes including the coal mines. When the system from generator to retailer (the later selling electricity to households and businesses) was, or is, one firm, the business is now called a "gentailer"—one of the many new bits of jargon one needs to decipher to read electricity industry documents. The business model for large-scale hydro-electricity was no different. Governments owned the hydro-electric dams, pipelines and turbines and made economic decisions based on this model.

This integrated framework simplified managing the total business and its finances. In the case of coal-generated electricity, mining, generation, transmission and distribution were coordinated and hence each part of the integrated business faced certainty in terms quantities of electricity to be produced and prices to be charged. Everything was planned centrally, and prices set so to cover costs and generate income for the government owners.

As a "socialised" business it worked reasonably well, except there was not the degree of oversight required. Hence gold plating. This is how the Industry Commission viewed it. The question most economists leave unanswered is what psychological disposition comes into play if a lack of concern for efficiency takes hold? Are bigger and better poles and wires monuments to the electricity engineers as bridge and dam names are to politicians? Maybe.

The natural monopoly nature of transmission and distribution (the poles and wires) was a major underpinning of the old model. This monopoly situation means that a government has to either own or regulate the transmission and distribution of electricity if consumers are not to be either undersupplied or over-charged, these being the options available to monopolists. In this period, governments set tariffs (the prices charged to consumers) on the basis that the operational costs were covered and the capital costs paid over time in a planned manner; that is, the power stations and the poles and wires were paid for over their life-time by levying specific charges on electricity consumers. The other costs of the electricity delivered into one's home or business, that is as distribution and related services, were based on meter readings of the amount of electricity used.

Under this system there were two universal principles. One related to consumers. Governments designated electricity as "an essential service", and therefore deemed it should be priced the same regardless of where one lived in Australia, in the outback, in the Torres Strait or Sydney. Each State and Territory had, and continues to have, its own pricing rules based on notions of equity. Obviously, it is more costly to provide electricity to people back of Burke than for a resident of Fitzroy in Melbourne. The result of this approach to equity is subsidised electricity for the distant consumers.

There are two means of providing electricity to those far from the main grids: low voltage links extending out from the grid; or, when great distances prohibit this, diesel generators. Gas can play a role and increasingly small-scale solar and wind generators are being used in the outback and Torres Strait, either as stand-alone generators or supplements to diesel generators.

The other principle is that governments took it upon themselves to sell electricity at discounted prices to industries deemed deserving of government support. The aluminium industry stands out. State governments compete for smelters in their jurisdictions by offering cheap electricity. This is a prime example of governments not abiding by the free-market principles they espouse. The industries obtaining electricity under special deals (ones that the voter does not get to sanction or reject, even though it is the voters' coal, gas and water that generate the electricity) are the major uses of electricity. There are no similar deals for those using only small amounts of electricity. This lack of consistency muddies the waters when debate occurs around the pricing of electricity. The subsidies to the large consumers tend to be overlooked in the public debate.

Following, or in concert with, the Industry Commission recommendations some state governments privatised parts of their electricity businesses. Those that did not were afraid of voters' reactions to the privatisation of publicly-owned infrastructure. Governments are known to fall over the privatisation of publicly-owned assets. What was not understood by governments taking the privatisation route by putting the theories of neo-liberal economics into practice was that they were out of step with voters' attitudes. A salutary lesson was the rejection at the polls in 2012 of the Queensland Labor Party government led by Anna Blyth. It broke a promise that privatisation of public assets would not occur. No Queensland political party since then has suggested privatisation of publicly-owned assets, least of all electricity.

Notwithstanding the altered organisational and financial structure of the electricity enterprises in the period following the Industry Commission report, the economics of electricity generation, transmission and distribution remained relatively simple. Coal, gas and hydro-power were to remain the sources of generation. Electricity was fed into the existing grids. There were to remain a large number of electricity generators, most being power stations located near coal mines, a number of gas-fired electricity providers, and two major hydro-electricity producers plus some small ones. The coal-fired ones used, and continue to use, either black or brown coal, the latter producing more greenhouse gases per tonne than the former. As a consequence of different levels of net energy produced, plus the mixed ages of the power stations, some provide electricity cheaper than others.

As an aside, a matter of importance in looking to the future cost of coal-fired electricity, of 17 major coal-based power stations only three are under 30 years in age. Ages range from 55 to 11 years. The expected life of a coal-fired power station is between 45 and 60 years. Australia has a stock of old power stations. One third of these power stations will close due to age and cost of maintenance over the next 15 years. The end of the coal age in Australia is likely to be within the next 15 to 20 years.

The economic question on their retirement is: what source of electricity is the cheapest to produce? We come to the answer in due course.

Until the renewable electricity revolution took hold in the last decade (that is, before intermittency became an issue) electricity authorities were able to plan on the basis of reasonably reliable predictions of demand for electricity, not only on a time-of-day, daily and seasonal basis, but for next year and beyond. Both intermediate-term and long-term planning were also possible. We will come to see that the industry was not as good at forecasting demand as we expected it to be, and as consumers of electricity this is costing us.

The way the system worked was as follows. At peak times of the day (late afternoon-early evening, and in the morning the hour or two before homes emptied as work and school beckoned), more costly sources of electricity were fired up and brought on to cover the increased demand. These had to be easy to fire up. Gas and diesel-generated electricity met both criteria, costly and quick to fire up. Not as quick as hydro-electric power stations. The mature renewable electricity, hydro-electricity, played, and plays, a critical role in meeting peak demand as it is also easy to fire-up. It will come to play the dominant role as pumped-storage hydro-electricity in smoothing out the generation of electricity as more and more is produced by intermittent solar and wind power.

The long-term requirement was to plan the commissioning and decommissioning of coal mines and gas fields. In this past era, no new large-scale hydro-electric schemes were envisaged. Because extra pumped-storage hydro-electricity was not a consideration until very recently, it did not figure in future planning. Then in 2008, what would turn out to be as time passed, dramatic changes to the time-worn electricity model started to occur. We will come to those, but other factors warrant mention as a prelude.

First, the electricity providers discovered that they had miscalculated future demand. They predicted a greater increase than that which resulted. The less-than-anticipated demand was in part due to the installation of roof-top solar panels putting surplus electricity into the grid during the sunlit hours. Another factor was the adoption of electricity-saving lighting, white goods and electric appliances. Per capita demand for electricity decreased. However, total demand was not significantly changed due to immigration boosting the Australian population. All told, in a complex changing situation, the predictions of growth made by the industry did not eventuate. By the time this was realised much money had been spent on upgrading poles and wires. This drove the increase in electricity bills.

Yet another factor that changed market conditions was that gas on the domestic market was to become dearer. The price of gas is important. Gas is a conventional source of peak demand electricity. What happened was that overseas demand for gas had grown to the extent that to meet foreign contracts, the domestic market had "to give way", to pay higher prices. While an economist would say let price increases sort out who got to burn Australian gas, this was not how the public, stirred up by the media, understood the situation. The result was a call to quarantine gas for the domestic market. Notwithstanding considerable discussion in the popular media, some of it alarmist, it is not at all obvious that the gas "shortage" was a problem. It certainly was not for those gas exporters who had negotiated good deals, with the support of governments at both Commonwealth and State level.

Those who oversaw the electricity system were caught unawares by these events, although some should have been foreseen; in particular that householders would come to produce for their own use electricity generated by photovoltaic processes in roof-top panels and, to make matters worse for the traditional electricity suppliers, sell surplus electricity to a grid. The very same State and Territory government ministers who owned or at least had control over conventional electricity suppliers were the same people offering feed-in tariffs for intermittent solar and wind-powered electricity.

The State/Territory feed-in incentives were, and continue to be, augmented by other financial incentives provided to households and others who were (and are) willing to install renewable electricity sources. These incentives were, and are, provided under the Commonwealth government's small-scale renewable energy target (RET) scheme, whereby those who installed photovoltaic panels (or small-scale wind, hydro-electricity, or solar hot water systems) "create" certificates which have a dollar value attached to them. This amount is able to be subtracted from the fee the installer charges for the solar system if the certificate is given by the householder to the installer. It is a substantial amount, approximately one-third of the full cost of installing a normal size photovoltaic solar panel system on the roof of a house. Today, a solar system a householder pays about $6,000 for installed would be worth about $9,000 without the Commonwealth government subsidy.

This is the only real subsidy given to householders as the feed-in tariffs at the level offered today are clearly not greater than the wholesale price of electricity. In other words, an electricity wholesaler has to purchase electricity from some source, a coal-based power station, a gas-based power station, a hydro-electric generator or households selling their surplus, and the wholesaler should pay a market price. Only in the very early days when feed-in tariffs were introduced did they exceed wholesale prices.

Electricity retailers purchasing electricity from a grid to sell to consumers have an obligation under the government's RET scheme to supply a set amount of electricity generated by renewable sources; and obviously, less generated by fossil-fuels. They achieve this objective by purchasing the certificates created when a householder installs solar roof panels. In most cases, the suppliers simply reduce the cost to the householder installing a renewable electricity source. The final stage of these transactions is when the certificates are surrendered to the government's Clean Energy Regulatory. This system is discussed in more detail in a future chapter.

Combined, the incentives of feed-in tariffs and the RET scheme delivered as promised—and more. The number of installations of roof-top panels exceeded what governments and the electricity generators expected. It was an unanticipated success.

Today, a large number of Australian householders and small businesses are producers of electricity (in the electricity business jargon they are called "prosumers", derived from "producers" and "consumers). These are the folk who have led the solar electricity revolution. The electricity they produce and sell into a grid is called "distributed" electricity.

Another term you will encounter in the electricity industry documents is "dispatchable" electricity. This refers to electricity generated by fossil fuels, such as coal and gas as well as to hydro-electricity. In other words, it refers to electricity capable of 24/7 dispatch and utilisation. And yet another term is "supercritical" coal-fired power stations. The one at Brigalow on the Darling Downs, known as Kogan Creek, is a relatively new (commencing operations in 2007) supercritical power station. It operates at higher pressure and temperature than conventional coal-fired power stations and hence is more efficient in converting coal into energy while producing less greenhouse gases than the conventional power stations. Another positive attribute is that it is air-cooled and consequently uses 90 per cent less water than the conventional power stations. Somehow the word "supercritical" is supposed to encompass all these characteristics.

We are not responsible for the amount of confusing jargon that is used in the electricity business. We take the view that electricity transmitted and distributed by a grid is distributed! And dispatchable is in common English that which can be … well, dispatched regardless of when or by whom. We have no clue as to how "supercritical" became one word and what is "critical" about it. There is enough confusion in the rapidly changing electricity business without adding to it by inventing new language.

Looking to the future, the extent of change in the production of electricity is going to be more dramatic than what we have experienced so far. An increasing number of households, small industries, community centres, schools and remote agricultural enterprises desiring to reduce their electricity bills will install photovoltaic roof top panels or, at the community-level, build small, ground-mounted solar farms. The decreasing cost of solar electricity leads inevitably to this conclusion.

Today, roof top solar panels make financial sense without subsidies, although there are valid economic reasons to keep the subsidies as they go some way in recognising that global warming will eventually result in damage costs and anything that reduces the quantity of greenhouse gas is a benefit. There is a rapid acceleration in building large-scale solar farms and wind farms. Large industries where they have not already moved to source their own electricity from their own manufacturing system (such as sugar cane mills using bagasse as a fuel for electricity generation) are investigating the economic gain by going off grid.

As we write, one can travel Australia and see operating solar farms, others under construction, and the same applies to wind farms. While wind farms are not the focus of this book, we must make mention of their rapid growth. Wind farms and the individual turbines (the modern name for a windmill) will continue to become larger and larger. Today, the largest solar and wind farms are of utility scale, meaning they are competitive in electricity output with conventional coal or gas power stations. They are also competitive in cost. To replace an existing coal-fired power station costs more than building a solar or wind farm with the same electricity capacity. Only the very old coal-fired power stations, if their capital cost has been paid for by consumers in previous years, can produce electricity cheaper than the renewables and then only until they, like very old "clunker" cars, are not worth repairing and maintaining.

In the past three years we have witnessed old, high-profile coal-fired power stations close. This has generated considerable debate in the media. Had there not been the solar revolution to blame these closures they would have been accepted as the normal state of affairs. Given the age profile we reported above, we expect more closures in the near future and others will follow in due course.

What commenced as an individual household cost-saying-cum-environmental concern has turned into a much wider and deeper change in electricity generation. If the change continues—and the momentum is with it—solar power plus the other two legs of the renewable revolution, wind and pumped-hydro, will come to replace the fossil-fuelled electricity generators. We are in the transitional phase and some major problems have to be solved on the way. Some very significant decisions are awaiting to be made. In this context doing nothing would be a likely disastrous decision, with uncertain outcomes. Due to what have become known as the "climate wars" (alternatively the "electricity war"), doing something is proving very difficult. These matters are for elaboration in future chapters.

Revolutions, whether industrial, technological or political tend to have their own twists and turns. I know of no supporter of a revolution who has got its trajectory and end state right. The best we can do is apply the basic principles and laws of economics in seeking to make sense of the solar electricity revolution.

While integration of the various sources of electricity remains a major challenge, there are those, both households and businesses, who have taken the solar revolution to another level. They have gone "off grid" or "beyond the meter", to introduce more industry jargon. In this case there is no public policy matter to be resolved. If stand-alone, off-grid electricity producers, whether they are sugar cane mills, cotton farms, mines or small rural communities, do not seek to sell any excess electricity into a major grid they can go about their business unnoticed—except by the grid operators who look on enviously. The off-grid households and businesses will not only serve their own economic interests through using a free fuel, but they will be doing their small part in helping thwart the global threat of climate change.

We must take notice of a mid-2018 report by the International Energy Agency (IEA), in which it reported that "off-grid private solar power is likely to be the key to the future of electricity globally"; followed by: "Bundling of off-grid renewables with efficient appliances and lighting gives households better quality energy services at a substantially lower cost, making off-grid access more affordable and reliable" (reported in the *Australian*, 3 July 2018). When the IEA makes a statement as profound as this, we need to take notice.

At present in Australia, the numbers "off-the-grid" are not large and are generally in remote locations or are associated with specialised industries that have available the resources to fuel their own electricity generation, such as the sugar mills using bagasse. As stories of successful off-grid solar electricity generation spread, we would expect what development economists call a "demonstration effect" and going off-grid will become more popular. However, off-grid "prosumers" are not the main story in Australia at present.

As the number of renewable electricity producers, both solar and wind, increases and they produce increasing amounts of electricity to sell into a grid, the search for seamless integration into the existing grids is paramount. As we expect there to be a number of years during the transition to a totally renewable electricity future and hence continued reliance on fossil-fuel generated electricity for a part of the total demand, we cannot sit back and hope for a solution to the integration of electricity sources. A solution has to be engineered. A key element of the transition will be the construction of new grids and/or major extension of existing ones. This is a story we take up in due course.

Here it is important to return to the intermittency matter and summarise the key points. One way to go off-grid or purchase less electricity when the sun is not shining, is to purchase a battery. We find it worth noting that Alan Finkel, Australia's Chief Scientist, has recently declared that home batteries are "the next step" for inexpensive and reliable electricity. In his assessment he noted that "Australia was the biggest residential energy storage market in the world"; and empathised that home storage was "crucial to the future of Australia's electricity network" (*Courier Mail*, 7 July 2018). This is a powerful statement by an eminent expert.

The appropriate sized batteries for household use are on the market, but their cost is still too high for wide-scale uptake. However, prices continue to fall. At the time of writing, a battery for household purposes will cost between $3,000 and $8,000. Some are cheaper, but as is said "you get what you pay for". Scale economies and technological advances in battery technology are driving the price fall. How soon batteries become an essential complement to solar roof panels is a matter of guess work, but once they do we would expect a significant shift to off-grid households. How a shift to off-grid supply by a significant number of electricity users plays out for the non-renewable sector is an important question. Obviously, it will be supplying less electricity, and this could (we do not say will) impact on its economies of scale and therefore profits. Alternatively, the sector could seek to maintain its present income by increasing prices to consumers, but this would surely result in even more going off-grid and at a faster rate.

It needs to be recognised that batteries might not prove to be the only, or major, or long-term solution to storage of electricity. It is far too early in the electricity revolution to know. One can very easily become bogged down in considering the claims and counter claims of the supporters of, respectively, batteries, pumped-storage hydro-power, or thermal solar. That there are options is very welcome. And they can be combined as complementary sources of electricity.

Of the likely future developments, some have reasonably high probabilities of succeeding, others more "possibilities" than "probabilities". It is not simply a matter of deciding on a means, or a combination of means, of generating electricity, there is a necessity to improve on the operation of the grid, on interconnection, transmission and distribution. The technological optimists look forward to the development of a so-called "smart grid" which will be able to source electricity from a range of scattered sources, distribute it across large parts of the (connected) nation at the times of the day and night when it is in demand.

Technological developments, plus ever less expensive solar electricity and the acceptance that the future costs of climate change are simply too high to continue to ignore, suggest the eventual end of coal and gas-fired electricity. The day this results, we hesitate to guess. What we do know is the historical record of economic development. The evidence is that as societies made technological progress they abandoned an existing energy source for a better one (in both terms of availability and cost) while the old resource was still relatively plentiful but due to distance from consumers, costly. Price increases did much to bring forward the substitution. For example, wood was becoming more difficult to get in places of high demand, the rapidly developing economic powerhouses of the United Kingdom and western Europe during the Industrial Revolution and, hence, dearer when coal became the substitute. As another example, whale oil for lighting was clearly destined for a limited life, given the decline in whale harvests and the costs of scouring the world's oceans.

A rapid substitution of electricity generation modes is unlikely. It serves no purpose to get ahead of the technological feasibility and real-world public policy. With regard to the latter the most basic matter is whether or not our governments will price fossil fuels used for electricity generation (that is, coal, gas and diesel) to account for what economists call the "damage costs" of future climate change. The adjective "future" is important. How far into the future? Massive tracts of literature have been written about these expected future costs, and not for us to repeat here.

It would be a mistake for us to suggest that these costs, of whatever magnitude—itself a major unresolved question—are going to be incorporated into consumers' electricity bills in the near future. Any reader with knowledge of politics in Australia will recall the unsuccessful attempts to put a price on carbon emissions. Regardless of the wishes of some, coal will continue to be used for electricity generation for a substantial period. We would expect at least 12 or more years, making 2030 the earliest end date. Much will depend on the speed of building solar and wind farms to complement the roof top revolution, as well as pumped-storage hydro-electricity and advances in battery technology. That is, the ball is in the court of the challengers.

We expect that much coal will be left in the ground as a so-called "stranded asset" when its final day comes. The factors that will determine the future of coal are beyond the power of the coal miners and politicians who support them. At an international level, the arrangements that are made to control and reduce the emissions of greenhouse gases will have a major influence on the future of coal mining worldwide. We note that the International Panel on Climate Change is presently struggling to make progress. On the other hand, we are aware of (and take on face-value) the commitments by European governments and those of China and India to pursue accelerated transition from fossil fuels. These aspirations will, ultimately, be reflected in formal international agreements.

The relative costs of the various electricity-generating fuels are more than likely than international agreements to be the major driver of substitution. The cost advantages that already exist for the non-renewables suggest that, unless "carbon capture and storage" can be made economic and very quickly (so as not to miss the boat), coal and the other fossil fuels are approaching retirement. It would be doing a disservice to coal, to leave unrecognised its role in human development. Hence, a digression which is a smidgen of history.

Coal has had a remarkable history, a very long and varied life in the service of humans. As a fuel to produce steam in electricity-generating powerhouses it had a short life. It had to wait for a breakthrough in electricity generation in the late nineteenth century. Only recently have we come to identify coal's downsides. It was used for heating when our ancestors lived in caves and used as fuel in Bronze Age China. Come to more recent times and we have discovered from archaeological evidence that coal was used in Britain in Roman times. Much later, coal came into its own as the European forests were dramatically depleted due to the use of wood for cooking, heating and building, including building ships to sail on the high seas. In the period of the first wave of colonisation (following Christopher Columbus' successful journey to the Americas), and ships sailed the seven seas without fear of dropping off the edge of the world, ship-building added to the demands on European forests.

By 1600 most of the southern English forests had been felled. An interesting fact is that when our ancestors started to use coal they found that it was superior to wood. Coal burned hotter and cleaner than wood charcoal. As a consequence of this attribute, coal gained favour. Importantly for the establishment of the Industrial Revolution in Britain, coal was found near the surface and hence was inexpensive to mine. Otherwise it was "free", no need to pay as was necessary in acquiring wood from a forest owner in Norway.

Consider the economics an English industrial enterprise faced in acquiring energy: wood from distant Norway or coal at your doorstep, and very cheap labour to dig and cart it. Much labour was provided by the poorest of the poor, rural desperate peasant children forced into the cities by the closure of the farmland commons. In the sheer desire to survive children dragged the coal-laden carts out of the underground mines. If this all too recent history is forgotten, it can be rediscovered it in the works of Charles Dickens, Friedrich Engels and Elizabeth Barrett Browning.

Steamships came to replace sail in the transport of the raw materials from the "new world" to the factories of the "old world" and returned (backfilled) with manufactured goods. On land, railways replaced horse-drawn wagons. Not only did the new manufacturing industries benefit, so did people on the move in search of a better future. The migration of European people who populated America at the end of the 19th–early 20th centuries benefitted greatly from relatively rapid steamship travel, and when in America railroad transport. Trains were fed coal by the shovel loads. This was still the case during the early part of my life in suburban Brisbane. The advice given to school-age travellers: "Don't lean out of the train window, otherwise coal grit will lodge in your eyes".

In the 1880s, coal came to be used to generate electricity and since then has remained the dominant fossil fuel used for this purpose. As an aside, we ought not to think of coal as "unnatural" as some who attempt to divide the world into "natural" equating to "good", and "unnatural" equating to "bad" do. Coal is as natural as the World Heritage Gondwana Rainforests in the Gold Coast and Byron Bay hinterlands. In fact, the abundant coal in Australia was formed out of the magnificent forests that surely most have covered large parts of the Australia component of the super continent known as Gondwana.

Life of all forms is brought into being by the combination of life-generating and life-supporting processes driven by the sun. Coal was originally living plants brought to life and nurtured by the sun. These forms of life die, decompose, get buried, squashed underneath the outer layer of the world that we live in. Coal is formed by this process; dead plants become a rock-like carbon source. And oil and gas are simply other forms of carbon that we burn to produce energy. Notwithstanding the downsides that we have come to recognise only recently, coal served humankind very well over the past 100 years or more.

We have found the means to short-circuit the process of waiting millions of years for decaying matter to eventually become coal which can be dug up and burned. We can now go directly to the sun by installing solar panels, and we can turn to the indirect force of the sun for yet other sources of electricity, wind and falling water. These brief comments must suffice as our recognition of coal in its final days.

Economics is, we argue, the most important driver in replacing coal with renewable sources of electricity. There should be no surprise in this as both sides of the "left-right" ideological divide recognise economics as the driving force of society. As we have noted, it is cheaper today to obtain electricity from a utility-size solar or wind farm than from a new coal-fired power station. For householders and others who go "off-grid" (with solar panels and batteries and no feed-in tariffs as a benefit), free electricity comes within five years. This we will discuss in a coming chapter.

Here we have cause to expand on economics. There is in play today a revolution in economic practice that has been a long time coming. It helps make renewable, non-carbon electricity an even better proposition. The long time we mention is near to 100 years. Some might suggest that on this basis economists are very slow learners, and there could be some truth in that. Nobel Prize-winning economist Gunnar Myrdal uses the term "inertia" to describe the progress in economics. To that we have no adequate response other than "better late than never".

The issue has been to get practitioners of economics when doing their sums for cost-benefit analyses to include costs that are not borne by either the producer or consumer. These are the economists' externalities. Arthur Pigou published the seminal work on externalities in the 1920s. At last recognition has come.

There are two main ways of—excuse the jargon, but it sort of resonates—"internalising externalities"; otherwise making the polluter pay. One way is by the writing of a law that prohibits the release of pollutants. In this case an upstream factory owner who has been emitting pollutants into a river flowing by will build a pond into which the pollutants will be directed and allowed to settle, and then taken away to be disposed of safely. The widgets and gadgets produced in the factory would cost the consumer more due the factory owner's additional, but justified cost.

The other method is for governments to impose a pollution tax, generally called an environmental tax or eco-tax (sometimes a Pigouvian tax). For the tax to do its allotted job, there has to be a close correlation between consumption of a widget and the pollution caused by its manufacture. If there is, a tax has to be high enough to result in a reduction in consumer purchases and consequently a reduction in pollution. Setting the magnitude of this tax would at best involving "educated guesswork". Obviously, for some manufacturing processes emitting dangerous pollutants, the tax would have to be incredibly high and it would be simpler to prohibit release of the pollutant.

How high would a greenhouse gas (carbon tax) have to be to stop serious damage from climate change? Sorry to say we do not know, although we can refer to the major research effort made by Lord Nicholas Stern some years ago, in 2006. For those with an inclination to explore this matter the *Stern Report: The Economics of Climate Change* is 700 pages of data, analysis and recommendations worth reading. Stern thankfully puts the discussing in English not the mathematics that economists far too often—and unnecessarily—resort to. Stern indicated that the damage cost of a tonne of carbon dioxide emitted could be as high as US$85. More recently Stern, joined by Nobel Prize winning economist Joseph Stiglitz, argued that by 2030 there would need to be a carbon tax of US$100/tonne if global warming was to be held to an increase of 2 degrees centigrade.

This increase is considered to be the "safe" level, beyond which some very serious concerns arise.

Based on the scientific evidence so far gathered, the real cost of using fossil-fuel-based electricity in the future will prove to be considerably higher than what we pay for this electricity today. We also know that as time passes, and more and more greenhouse gases accumulate in the atmosphere and weather patterns change and sea levels rise, greater damage will be done: more severe cyclones; more, and more severe droughts; increased human health impacts due to heat waves and the spread of tropical diseases; increased loss of biodiversity as in the case of corals on the Great Barrier Reef. There are numerous other examples of future damages that climate change is expected to generate. In noting that, we recognise that there could also be positive impacts of climate change in certain regions of the world, for example, the ability to grow tropical crops in what was previously a cold climate.

Here is another economic factor taking us to a future of renewable electricity generation. It is its declining cost, due to advancements in technology and economies of large scale production. This applies to both solar panels and wind turbines. This was the story of solar hot water panels. There was a 20-year lag between development and the start of a householder driven demand for solar hot water. The history of technological advancement shows that it runs ahead of market demand. In the case of solar-generated electricity, optimistic expectations have proven to be correct, but only in the past decade. With the evidence of sustainable sales, bankers are financing the manufacturers of solar technologies and those constructing solar farms are finding financial backers. But it has not always been as easy as it is today. Trials and tribulations are a key part of the story.

There is a particular Australian cultural characteristic which has helped the growth of solar technologies. Australians have a proven propensity to be eager early adopters of most things new and are particularly keen on the most recently available technology. Solar electricity is proving to be no different. Good science and, for those living in the sunniest places on earth, good fortune have come to be on the side of inventors, manufacturers and consumers of solar electricity.

There is yet another economic factor to consider. Whether you are an owner of a house considering the installation of a few solar panels, a community keen on a small-scale wind farm, a farmer wanting cheap electricity to pump water, or a major infrastructure developer contemplating building a utility-scale solar or wind farm, the cost of borrowed money to build and/or install used to be a hurdle. Interest rates were high. In living memory, the cost of borrowed money (or the opportunity cost of using your own money) has not been as low as it is today. Of course, all businesses benefit from cheap money, but it is particularly attractive for householders and small firms.

In summary, what is favouring solar photovoltaic electricity generation is technological advancements. This, as will be discussed in a coming chapter, is a matter of pride for Australian scientists. There are the economies of large-scale production (thanks to low-cost labour in China where panels are made), cheap finance, and the various attempts by governments to combat—if only marginally—the future costs to society of climate change. The latter include mandatory targets for electricity produced by clean technologies, and feed-in tariffs for householders selling excess solar electricity to the grids. These are the so-called subsidies that the climate change deniers attack. We note that these incentives go some way to correct the future costs that are predicted to result from the pollution of the atmosphere, and if they are called subsidies they deserve to be called "good subsidies", or compensating (off-setting) subsidies— truthful language.

The success of feed-in tariffs in inducing the uptake of photovoltaic roof top panels is evident in the suburbs of Australia's cities. It is argued that they have proven too successful for governments. That is, householders have been keener to take advantage of them, for both personal economic reasons and a concern for the environment, than was expected. As Chris Goodall in his book *The Switch* (2016, p. 126) comments "governments around the world remove renewable subsidies as fast as they can without too much embarrassment". It is, or should, be embarrassing to take away something that was very heavily promoted not long before.

The argument made by governments when they have removed or reduced the value of feed-in tariffs is that the cost to the household of installing photovoltaic panels has dropped to such an extent that the incentive provided by a subsidy is no longer needed. This, on the face of it, is true. However, the incentives provided to renewable electricity were not simple an "infant industry" proposition; that is, providing assistance until the industry could sustain its self. Rather, they were considered to be the "other side" of a carbon tax. If it was, as the case in Australia, too politically difficult to impose a carbon tax, the least a government could do is help promote a "clean-green" solution.

As we approach the end of this overview chapter, it seems appropriate to ever so briefly note the start of electricity generation in Australia. The year 1882 is taken to be the year that electricity came to Australia. Here we are putting aside events such as the football matches played under arc lights at the Melbourne Cricket Ground in 1879, and some other interesting pioneering adventures with lighting. It was in 1882 that the parliament house of the Queensland colonial government was lit by electricity. Following this there were eight electric lights installed in Queen Street, Brisbane. The power was generated by a 10 horse-power engine in a foundry in neighbouring Adelaide Street.

Other than these interesting events, we have not the space to discuss in any depth the history of electricity in Australia. The one fact to note, and this is evident to people interested in the built heritage of their towns and cities, is that small power stations where built in the suburbs, not in distant locations near coal mines as is the case to-day. The central business districts had their own power station; for example, there was the Spencer Street Power Station in Melbourne to provide electricity to illuminate the streets of the inner city of Melbourne.

For a moment or two let us imagine being at the MCG on the first occasion football was played under lights.

2.

Taking the Heat Out of the Debate: A "No Regrets" Revolution

TOR HUNDLOE AND KEELEY HARTZER

The solar electricity revolution arrived in Australia in two forms: first in the form of photovoltaic solar panels on roof tops and, second in the form of on-the-ground solar farms, both providing electricity directly from the sun. It would be remiss of us to neglect the much earlier innovation, solar hot water heaters. Their success led to experimentation on solar panels.

The word "revolution" is chosen deliberately. A revolution is a far-reaching, radical change from what went before. A successful revolution results in permanent change—at least until the next revolution. When we think of revolutions we tend to think of political revolutions, such as the American Revolution, the French Revolution and the Russian (Soviet) Revolution. None of these were permanent in the sense that most of their key features have remained in place. Two ultimately failed (the French and the Russian) while the other has deviated from many of its fundamental foundation principles.

The revolution that interests us is technological and economic in nature. In other words, it is a step in the material progress of humankind. It is about unlimited, free electricity, free in the sense that the "fuel" is free. Converting it to electricity is not free. Throughout history humans have struggled to invent—and eventually achieve—the means of reducing human effort. That is, substituting non-human energy for human energy, the latter derived from the food we eat. Fire came first. It was used to cook foods which uncooked were inedible. We ate more, we became stronger and more productive. But, human energy had to be exerted to gather wood to fuel the fires.

Our forebears invented (discovered by accident?) farming. As time went by, beasts of burden, as we came to call them, came to substitute for human energy in pulling ploughs through paddocks to be cultivated, and when crops were ready for market these beasts of burden provided the "horse power" to transport them. Of course, we needed to use our energy to feed the animals, to train them and to drive them. We had not escaped the use of human energy, but we were using it for less arduous tasks and achieving much more. As time went by our thinkers and inventors (being fed from the agricultural surplus without expending their own effort in farming) accumulated knowledge. They came to understand the power of wind and water and to use these gifts of nature our ancestors had the job of inventing and constructing apparatus that could be moved by wind and water—sailing boats and water mills. And so on throughout history humans have sought out ever more efficient and less costly forms of energy. We must truncate the ancient history here lest too much space is taken up on the human journey.

The most significant change in human material circumstances came not much more than a century ago with the discovery of the means of mining and utilising the embedded energy in the fossil fuels. We came to use them to produce electricity, to power our vehicles, and to fire our furnaces. In terms of human history, it is but a tiny time that has passed since the commencement of the fossil fuel era. Today it faces a powerful challenger, with the evidence building in favour of the challenger.

Depending on how the challenger develops, one possibility is that it could make every household, school, hospital, shopping centre, factory and office block the generator of its own electricity. The fuel would be free as noted, not have to be dug from the ground. If the fuel is sun light, we know the sun shines only part of the day and it is not of the same intensity in all parts of Australia; and there are periods where rain falls for days on end. To overcome this problem of intermittency the solar revolution will need to call on its formidable partners, the infant wind farm industry and the very mature and powerful hydro-electric industry. The latter is in the process of a massive expansion of its pumped-storage capacity. Hydro-electricity is a twenty-four hour a day, seven days a week electricity. It is the most likely solution to solve the intermittency problem.

Note that in arguing that a significant transformation of electricity generation is underway , we have made little mention of global warming, no unrelenting condemnation of coal and the other fossil fuels with their greenhouse emissions; no case being made that the solar revolution is absolutely necessary to save the planet from over-heating. Of course, it will do that when it puts the fossil fuels out of business in the electricity industry. But for readers who are ambivalent about climate change, you would be wrong to view the solar revolution as nothing more than an attack on coal. If that was all it was, who knows it could lose out to coal. No, the solar revolution is first and foremost an economic revolution. Human history is the record of one successful economic revolution after the other. We recognise that there are gaps of hundreds of years when much, not all, of human society regressed in a "dark age", but this does not invalidate the general case of on-going improvement. The solar revolution is the latest economic revolution and we are privileged to live through and describe its early days.

We commenced our analysis by asking (ourselves in the first instance) would we welcome solar electricity even if we had no concerns that climate change was going to make the world a poorer place with less food, more disease, loss of life, and destruction of property? To answer that question, we had to think economics. For the sake of our inquiry we assumed that there was no build-up of greenhouse gases and consequently no damage costs in the future as a reason to change our source of electricity. On that basis, would we with the scientific breakthroughs in silicon-based photovoltaic solar panels and their ever-decreasing cost not make solar-based electricity our future?

Would our fellow Australians accept a renewable electricity future for one simple reason: that it will provide them with electricity cheaper than the sources they presently rely on? In our ever so brief recourse to history, ancient and modern, we came to conceptualise this question from the viewpoint of economic historians. We believe the answer is "yes".

To put it succinctly, humans have not as far as the records tell us rejected a better economic deal when it has appeared. This has been the case notwithstanding the fact that at the start of an economic revolution there have been losers. When radical changes in technology and modes of production occur those who made their living from the superseded technology are in economic trouble. This explains, in part, the arguments against solar electricity. But if the majority benefit, and they recognise that there are unfortunate losers and compensate them, progress results.

In summary, the revolution in electricity generation from coal and gas to the renewables is in the first place a result of good science. However, its long-term success is destined to be determined by economics. A concern for the future threatened by climate change could be the least important driver. This is not to dismiss or downgrade this concern, it is simply to argue that if solar-generated electricity trumps coal-based electricity on economic grounds, the winner is solar. Those who wish to deny climate change can continue to argue and it won't matter as the solar revolution will continue regardless. And the threat of climate change is diminished.

The renewable electricity revolution has no clearly identified speed of progression; therefore, at the present it is not possible to be adamant as to the time when we can say "we have arrived", when will we declare the end of coal (and the other fossil fuels). We suggested a possible date in the previous chapter. However, that we are well and truly on a journey is obvious. If recognition in the eminent journal of economic affairs *The Economist* is taken as a sign that we have started on something revolutionary and far-reaching, the tide has well and truly turned.

The February 25th, 2017 edition carries an article headed "A world turned upside down". The sub-title elaborates: "Wind and solar energy are disrupting the century-old model of providing electricity". The following reference is made to Australia, even though it is dated (much happens quickly in the solar electricity field) the message is clear.

> Consider Australia. It has 1.5 m households with solar cells on their roofs. There are a number of reasons for this. It is a sunny place; installing pvs [photovoltaic solar] was until recently generously subsidised; and electricity bills are high.

Here is recognition that solar-based electricity is cheaper than fossil-fuel generated electricity.

Above we mentioned that fossil fuels as our prime energy source, including generating electricity, have been around for not much more than a century. And so is the case of electricity itself. The electric generator was invented in the late 1800s. This helped speed up the growth of the later stages of the Industrial Revolution. The benefits were not only evidenced in factory production but in commerce, farming, entertainment, agriculture and work in and around the house. Thomas Edison writing in 1912 in the magazine *Good Housekeeping* called electricity "the greatest of all handmaidens" due to the ever-increasing array of electric appliances used in middle class households. It took decades to transform housework completely. Not so industry. The "flick-of-the switch" instant mechanical power changed manufacturing processes in ways we had not been able to imagine before it arrived.

Imagining futures can be fun or serious business for futurists and science-fiction writers. None image the unexpected. For those of us who have lived through the information and technology revolution, a number of the recent changes it introduced were not imaginable. Maxwell Smart's shoe phone was a bit of fun—"your shoe is ringing"—but we suspect those who grew up watching this television program did not image our modern "smart" phones. We are making the point that electricity opened doors we did not know existed. Now that we have discovered them, we want to keep them open. And we are seeking the cheapest way of doing so.

It pays to be reminded how new the newcomer, solar generated electricity, is. The first residence to be powered by solar electricity (a combination of photovoltaic and solar-thermal energy) was built by the University of Delaware in

1973. It was appropriately called Solar One. On the other hand, solar heating of water for domestic use and heating of buildings has a much longer history. The modern version of a solar hot water system is a simple panel that first appeared in numbers on Australian roofs in the 1970s. However, in a primitive form it was introduced in the 1950s in north Queensland. While solar hot water heaters became popular in the sunniest parts of Australia throughout the late 1970s, into the 1980s and beyond, solar-powered electricity in the form of roof top panels did not become noticeable until 10 years ago.

The most observable feature of the solar electricity revolution in Australia confronts us as we travel around our major cities and towns. Easier than identifying the revolution from on the ground, fly into a city airport and as your aircraft descends view the roof tops below. Ten years ago, the view from an aircraft's window was of red or metallic grey roofs, suburb after suburb. Today, navy-blue or black panels, shining, some glaring back at you if the angle of the sun makes this possible, sit on one-in-five roofs, and in some Brisbane suburbs on one-in-two roofs. As the capital of the "Sunshine State" this is not unexpected.

As already noted, the household solar electricity revolution benefitted from a "kick start" via government policies (renewable energy targets) and financial incentives (feed-in tariffs for sale of surplus electricity). In recent times the revolution has become householder driven due to the dramatic decrease in the cost of installing roof top panels. Take notice of the number of different cost curves produced by solar electricity experts over the past decade and you see a curve dropping at a 45 per cent angle. This is a fast-downhill ride over a very short time!

If a revolution is to sustain itself it needs to be "bottom up"; that is, based on the attitudes of, and willingness to spend by, household electricity users; that is us. Top down revolutions are not necessarily sustainable. This one started as "top down" but has become "bottom up".

There can be value in an initial top down approach. In formal economic terms this concept is based on the need for an "infant industry" to get a helping hand to reach maturity. For some decades now, Australian national governments, regardless of political persuasion, have rejected the infant industry concept. This means that when the renewable electricity business got government support, this ran counter to the prevailing economic ideology. Providing subsidies to any sector of the economy was known as governments "picking winners". As we were not privileged to sit in on cabinet meetings, we do not know what arguments were put that over-rode the conventional wisdom. It was an important win by those who drove it.

The reasons why some European countries with much less sunshine than Australia got the jump on Australia in developing their renewable electricity sector was their rejection of laissez-faire economics. They remained faithful to the notion of helping infant industries get established. They were in favour of a pro-government economic philosophy and trusted expert bureaucrats to be more, or just as, capable of picking winners as their private sector counterparts! These European countries and their experience are subject matter to for a future chapter.

We quote Millar and Minchin (2009) in support of our argument. They write: "in Europe, seemingly absent here, [is] a belief that elected governments have the right to make big, transformative decisions in what is perceived to be the good of the public, economy and environment".

The ongoing political fight over Australia's future electricity sources, a matter we will come to, is in large part driven by the different political ideologies and attitudes to climate change. If one does not believe in the threat of global warming, solar-generated electricity is not warranted. This is their view. However, if renewable electricity is the cheapest electricity on earth, what these people think is irrelevant. Economists understand that what people do, particularly if they purchase certain products, is all the evidence needed to illustrate success in the market.

Figure 1 illustrates the dramatic increase in roof top photovoltaic installations in Australia. The diagram shows that until 2009 there was very little uptake of roof top panels, but from then on the yearly increase has been rapid, becoming ever faster in the period in which we write. Electricity generation is measured in Megawatts (MW). There is no need to be familiar with this measurement to appreciate the steep slope of the curve. It approximates a 60-degree upward slope.

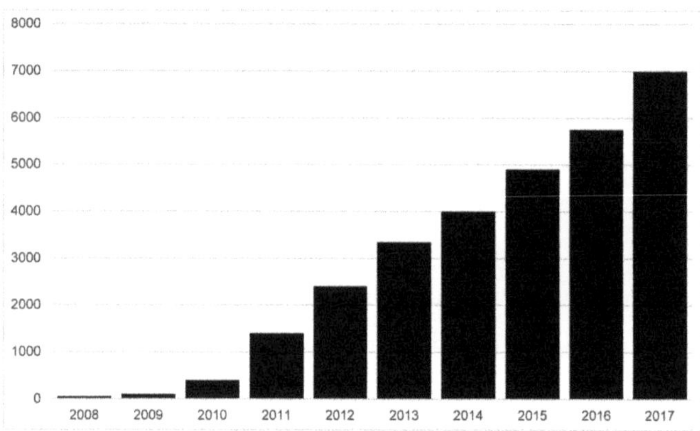

Figure 1. Cumulative Roof Top Photovoltaic Capacity. Source: Australian PV Institute

As a digression, for those who are yearning to know, one MW of electricity capacity is roughly equal to the energy capacity of one-and-a-third horses (what old-timers call "horse power"). Very larger trucks still advertise their enormous engine strength in hundreds of horsepower. We were advised not to use this measurement as in this era very few people would relate to it. Not convinced, we inquired of a number of younger folk and discovered a significant number of them (mainly females) related to horse power. They rode horses, fed them, groomed them and a few competed in equine events. These people have a good idea of the power of a horse but had no idea what a Megawatt was until we compared it to the strength of a horse. As educators, we know that non-experts relate to that which is material (physical world phenomena and experiences) rather than the measures used in physics and chemistry.

Figure 2 illustrates the strength of the Australian solar panel revolution in comparison to comparable overseas countries.

It illustrates that Australian households are world leaders. In addition to panels on households, an increasing number are being installed on commercial and public buildings. For example, the South Australian government has forged ahead with photovoltaic panels on its Parliament House, the South Australian Museum and the Art Gallery, plus hundreds of schools. The State of South Australia is setting out to be the nation's leader, determined to have 50 per cent of its electricity provided by renewables by 2025. It is likely to achieve this much earlier.

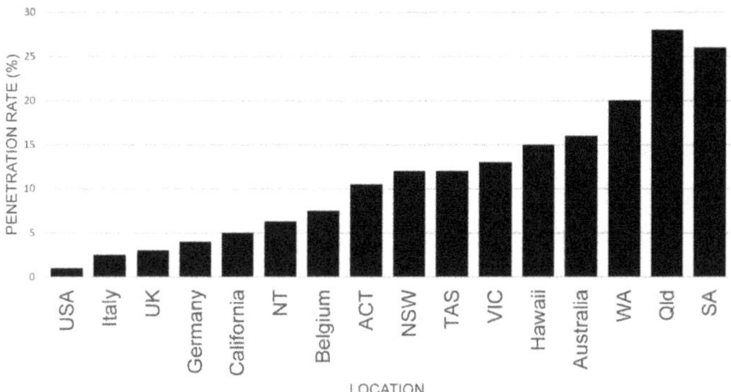

Figure 2. Penetration Rate of Photovoltaic Roof Top Panels. Source: Based on 'Independent Review into Future Security of the NEM', Dept. of Env., 2016

Attempts to make the comparisons between the sources of electricity simple, to help the householder and society in general make evidence-based decisions, are common place. Technical types are prone to do it in terms of the relative cost of kilowatt hours for the competing fuels, in a method called the "levelised cost of electricity" (LCOE). However, this term and the concept (except in a very general way) was not used by householders we interviewed. They had their preferred method or relied solely on those they considered experts and they tended to be installers of solar panels.

We found that those considering installing panels did one of three things (they are not mutually exclusive): take the word of a firm installing panels; obtain three quotes from installers; undertake an individual analysis. The latter involved everything from relatively sophisticated analysis to a back-of-a-postage-stamp calculation.

One couple we met with were Sonny and Daisy Billson (not their real names for the purpose of privacy). They live on the Sunshine Coast with two school age children. Sonny is a professional landscape architect running his own business. Daisy is a school teacher. We asked them how they approached making a decision to install solar panels.

The first thing they considered was the up-front expense of installing solar panels and an inverter. They had a small savings sitting in a bank earning a small amount of interest. If they withdrew it from the bank and installed solar panels would they be better off? This is the question they asked themselves. They had a reasonable expectation of how their "investment", as they called it, would work out.

From the day the installation took place they believed that a reasonable proportion of their electricity was going to be free; and in addition to that benefit, they expected that they would earn money from the sale of excess electricity during the sunniest part of the day. Their net benefit would be the sum of the money saved from purchasing less electricity plus the amount of money obtained from selling their surplus into a grid. Over the life-time of solar panels (25 to 30 years) they expected, but were not sure, that a substantial sum of money would be saved. However, the needed to calculate the opportunity cost, what they would forgo if they used their small savings to have solar panels installed. Figure 3 illustrates the way roof top solar electricity works with purchases and sales to a grid. Purchases are made from the grid when the sun is not shining, and sales are made to the grid when excess electricity is generated throughout the sunny period of the day.

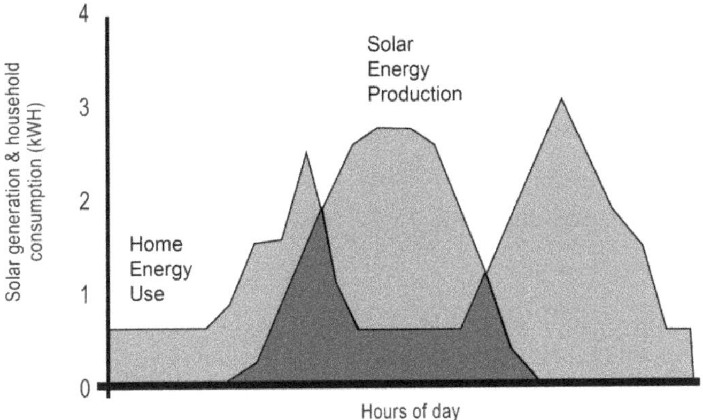

Figure 3

Before we summarise the Billson's story, we need to make abundantly clear that there is no typical Australian household; that is, the truism that every house is different holds. On a geographical scale, we could be comparing dwellings in the wet tropics, to those in the dry interior, to those in the snow fields, to those in Melbourne (which is said to experience four seasons in one day). Melbourne averages 46 sunny days and 139 partly sunny days per year; Brisbane averages 126 sunny days and 134 partly sunny days per year; Bendigo is not much different from Brisbane with 110 sunny days and 150 partly sunny days, while Ballarat has only 57 sunny days and 162 partly sunny days; Perth has 144 sunny days and 121 partly sunny days. Some of the differences are quite marked.

At the local scale we find houses with roofs partly shaded by neighbours' trees, to ones completely free of shading. In bushy suburbs, there are houses where possums roam the roofs of a night and will sleep under the panels through the day. By itself that is not a problem. The problem is possums chewing through the cables. Anecdotal reports of the "possum problem" have unlucky householders replacing panels within a few years of installation. Then there is the fact that there is no typical usage of electricity, or when it is used during the day. Many factors come into play. Significant ones are the number of people living in the house—if some are youngsters, their ages make a difference; the type and number of electrical appliances owned; and, simply attitudes the use of electricity.

Sonny and Daisy Billson explained their decision-making method for us. They had a quote of $5,000 for a roof top photovoltaic array of panels (capacity of 5 kW) plus inverter. This was an actual sum they spent in April 2018. If the solar package had not been purchased, this money would have earned interest, if only minimal, in a virtually risk-free investment. They worked on it earning 2.5 per cent per year. They built in inflation at 2 per cent per year. This means the "opportunity cost" of spending the money on solar panels rather than keeping it parked in safe place is 4.5 per cent per annum in nominal terms (2.5 per cent in real terms). This equates to $225 per year on their $5,000. They informed us that until now they spent the "dividend" each year as a "bonus", rather than reinvesting it and see it slowly grow. The items they purchased each year with this money would be foregone if the solar panels were installed. Sonny had taken a first-year economics subject as an elective in his degree and came to think the best thing he learned was the concept of "opportunity cost"—what is foregone if you do one thing not the other.

The next step for Sonny and Daisy was to account for the life span of the solar panels. They were confident with a 25-year life, as they had been told this is the industry standard; 30 years was a possibility. They had also been informed that as the panels age there would be some minor loss of electricity generated, and they would need to clean them every now and then. They could not estimate these small costs but were not concerned about them. And finally, they accepted that the panels would be only scrap value at the end of their life.

Daisy thought of paying for the solar installation over its life time in the same way as she had thought about the purchase of her first car when she was at university. On this basis, each year there would be an "outlay" of $200 (that is, $5000 divided by 25 years). On her thinking the solar installation would be worth $4,800 at the end of the first year, and by year 25 its value would be nought. This concept of an annual "loss" is easy to understand by reference to the purchase of a motor vehicle; it depreciates in value year-in, year-out, however the decrease in value of the vehicle is much more rapid and dramatic than that of solar panels. The Billson's arrived at a sum of $425 ($225 plus $200) that had to be "earned" each year by the solar array if it was to cover its depreciation (ultimately to reach zero scrap value). That is (discounting aside) they wanted to have $5,000 at the end of the period. And they had to cover the money that would have been earned had the amount spent on the panels been put in an interest-earning account (with the interest earned spent each year).

The panels earn their money by providing free electricity when the sun is shining and selling any surplus electricity to the grid (see Figure 3). However, from the money they saved and the money they earned they had to subtract the amount spent on purchasing electricity when the sun is not shining. If the Billson's became better off to the tune of $426 at the end of each year, they were in front, if only by one dollar per year. Of course, they wanted to do better than that.

They knew that they were paying about $1,700 per year on electricity. The Billson's then undertook a very difficult task of attempting to estimate the savings from their electricity bills if they installed solar panels. Like many people we interviewed they found their bill not detailed or explicit enough—or simply confusing because it was not in plain English, but rather used measures such as kilowatts per hour, not everyday language for anyone but experts. The Billson's went back to first principles, starting with their daily use of hot water, air conditioning, refrigeration and other major electrical appliances. The time of the day when these high electricity users were "on" mattered. Variations in use due to season and out-of-the-ordinary weather mattered. The more detailed their investigations became, the greater the number of variables they were forced to include. The results, even when averages were estimated or guesstimated and rounded, differed significantly for each alteration in a key variable. Their task became a major computational exercise, beyond their skills. And all before the different feed-in rates available to them became another variable.

To truncate the Billson's story here, swapped with different numbers—and having enjoyed the mental exercise involved—they turned to the solar panel guides available, there being quite a few. The results from consulting the guides suggested that some of the Billson's crucial estimates were consistent with the guides, but not all. The guides are based on a model and, therefore, a simplification of real-world cases. The Billson's final check was to have a solar panel installer prepare a specific assessment for their residence based on two different feed-in rates.

The installers started with a satellite image of their roof top (checking shading, orientation and slope); then studied their latest electricity bills; and, then questioned the Billson's seeking answers to questions about electricity use. The Billson's' 5-kW system, with a feed-in tariff of 16 cents/kWh was predicted to have paid back the $5,000 in just under three years. Feed-in tariffs have increased significantly from the low of 6 cents/kWh they reached when governments reduced them after the high initial offers.

What is most interesting is the payback period if the RET subsidy was withdrawn, a possibility as we write. For the Billson's this would increase their payback period to 5 years.

Yet, they would have another 20 to 25 years near free electricity for their use. There is no reason to believe that the Billson's' expectations won't be met. They should have no regrets.

We mentioned LCOE above. Because it is the favourite "metric" of the electricity industry folk, we need to put it into an economic perspective. What LCOE does is summarise the costs of the competing electricity generating technologies in cents per kilowatt hour. This seems sensible and is simple in theory. In practice the results are variable. Different analysts come up with different results for the same electricity source. There a number of reasons for this.

In practice the procedure does not make obvious certain key variables. Of course, one can undertake the analysis oneself and then the data plugged in is yours and one is not left guessing how future costs and benefits are being measured, or what is the discount rate applied. In the Billson story there was a deliberate decision to not discount future costs and benefits. Analysts, in particular economists, apply a discount rate in their calculations, and this means the savings on electricity bills in the far future are counted in cents not dollars. Discounting works against renewable electricity sources, a point we wish to empathise.

In Australia, households consume only one-third of the electricity produced, the remainder is used by industry and commerce. This means that the challenge of a significant reduction in greenhouse gases is a much more difficult task than covering the roof of every Australian residence with solar photovoltaic panels. This is where large utility-scale solar and wind farms will play the key role. The rapid rate at which they are being built has caught everyone by surprise.

In mid-July 2018, Audrey Zibelman, head of the Australian Energy Market Operator (AMEO), noted the "unprecedented rate of change" in the electricity industry and concluded with the assessment that as coal-fired power stations are retired—many are due for retirement—they can be "most economically replaced with a portfolio of utility-scale renewable generation, storage, distributed energy sources, flexible thermal capacity, and transmission". In its assessment, AMEO made the very important point that upgrading transmission capabilities to cater for this mix of sources is the first thing that needs to be done.

Here we introduce the first commercial solar farm in Australia, so to illustrate the difference in scale between an individual residence and 1,000 plus houses. The first commercial-scale solar farm had a very small 1 MW capacity (compared to a 5 kW household arrangement). It was opened as recently as 2011. It is situated just south of Alice Springs. It is called the Uterne Solar Power Station. Uterne means "bright sunny day" in the local Arrente (Indigenous) language. This power station, which feeds electricity into the Northern Territory grid, has since been expanded to near 5 MW capacity. This is enough to produce electricity for 1,100 homes and reduce carbon dioxide emissions by more than seven tonnes per year. Each little bit helps.

We will come to consider the potential for many more Uterne-type solar farms as well as the utility-styled ones. However, here we conclude this chapter by describing the transmission and distribution of electricity in Australia. The starting point is the world's longest interconnected grid. We have already introduced this as the east coast grid managed by the NEM. It is a synchronous electricity transmission line, spanning 5,000 km and venturing over five different States plus one Territory: Queensland, New South Wales, Victoria, South Australia, Tasmania and the Australian Capital Territory; that is, six cross-border connections. It consists of 40,000 km of transmission lines and cables. Its total capacity is about 54,500 MW. It serves 10 to 11 million homes and businesses. The day-to-day management of the NEM is undertaken by the Australian Energy Market Operator.

The NEM was formed in 1995 and began operating at the end of 1998; however, it was not until 2005 that Tasmania joined, and then it was not until 2006, when the under-sea cable (Basslink) was opened, that electricity could flow between Tasmania and the mainland. The NEM is the backbone of electricity transmission for most of Australia and, hence, we will have to work with it—extend and upgrade it were necessary—to meet the technical requirements of a truly integrated system. Major technological and economic challenges are involved in managing the intermittency that solar and wind-generated electricity has introduced. The search for solutions is being stymied due to political factors. This must not be allowed to continue.

However, regardless of the increasing difficulties in managing a distribution system designed around coal mines, the installing of solar panels on roofs will continue unabated.

With a payback period reduced to three years for an array of solar panels on household roofs, small business or community buildings such as schools, and a five-year payback without any subsidy, the "roof-top revolution" will continue to build on its already very strong rate of growth.

3.

In Search of a Policy

TOR HUNDLOE AND KEELEY HARTZER

In this chapter we pay attention to the policy settings on climate change and electricity generation. While the Australian public is "voting" in the electricity "market-place" in pursuit of a clean energy future by installing roof top solar panels, Australian governments face very difficult public policy decisions on climate change and related energy policies. The lack of concrete settled policies are the cause of a low level of certainty held by investors in the energy field. Nothing is more difficult for investors to second guess government decisions. Investors are by their very nature comfortable with risk to which they can assign probabilities, but shy away from uncertainty under which they don't know what they don't know.

The problem is not that there are not, or have not been, formal policies, some embedded in statutes, rather it is that with a change of government existing policies are scuttled. In fact, for this to occur does not require a change of government, simply a change of the leader of the governing political party. That the renewable electricity revolution in Australia is progressing as strongly as it is, given the political circumstances, is evidence of a very strong public commitment based on economic benefits. Take those away and we would be in the doldrums.

Most of the blame for the existing uncertainty can be sheeted home to governments at Commonwealth level. Only at this level has government the authority to agree to international approaches to act on climate change and follow up by legislating to first constrain and then go on to reduce greenhouse gas emissions. This can be done via so-called "carbon taxes", legislating for caps on emissions (aimed at the emitters of large amounts of the greenhouse gases), and/or providing powerful financial incentives to non-greenhouse gas emitting energy technologies. The States and Territories have a role in encouraging both householders and solar and wind farm operators. Where State and Territory governments own or oversee electricity retailers the governments can ensure that the feed-in tariffs on offer are fair in relation to the wholesale electricity produced from coal or gas.

Recent political history underscores the difficulty the Australian national government has had in dealing sensibly and consistently with climate change and energy policies. Who holds the position of Australian Prime Minister is determined, in large part, on that person's public views on climate change. Climate change politics has been, and remains, a roller-coaster ride in Australia. Much has been written on this topic, but because a lot is from conflicting viewpoints it is not helpful. Only the briefest sketch is presented here, enough to clarify the arguments.

It pays to go back in time as there were long periods of political agreement before the "climate wars" that we have endured for the past 10 years commenced. The first thing to note is that at the highest level, in both Australian political circles and in the scientific community, climate change was taken seriously from the time it became a major public issue in the late 1980s. In the lead up to the United Nations Earth Summit in Rio in 1992, the Commonwealth government initiated a public inquiry into the costs and benefits of reducing greenhouse gases. The then recently formed Industry Commission was given the task of conducting the inquiry. No climate change denier raised a voice or gave evidence. If deniers existed then (of this we have no evidence), they did not appear before the Commission to argue their case. It was some years before some in the media were to champion their cause and start the "climate wars".

In the early 1990s, there was scant understanding of the potential costs resulting from the building up of greenhouse gases in the atmosphere. Wide-scale, broad geographical assessments of possible changed climate conditions were made, so that in general terms it was possible to identify parts of the globe and parts of Australia likely to suffer in some form or other. Go to a fine geographical scale and much uncertainty existed. Would Australian agriculture face the loss of productivity in the already hot regions as they become hotter? Would these areas become dryer? What of the presently cold areas? Would tropical diseases spread south as the cooler climes warmed? Increased sea temperatures and sea levels where expected, but how soon would coral reefs become stressed? More damaging extreme weather events were predicted, but again where, when and how many were not able to be determined.

This lack of knowledge (lack of precision as to impacts where, when and of what magnitude) was to change, if only at the margin, as the world's climatologists and other scientist beavered away, and the International Panel on Climate Change synthesised the research results and developed "scenarios" with degrees of probability assigned to them. In Australia, CSIRO did sound research and the Bureau of Meteorology (BOM) took a serious interest in investigating climate change.

Notwithstanding the lack of scientific knowledge and little idea of how the rest of the world's nations were positioning themselves to deal with global warming, the Industry Commission put some important ideas out in the public arena. These included a strong case for carbon taxes and pollution permits, the latter being the basis of the so-called "cap and trade" approach. For the Industry Commission to be in support of taxes on pollution—regardless of the fact that this was a standard economic principle—sent a message to governments which could not be ignored, and which was going to cause much political trouble in the future.

The significance of the Industry Commission's greenhouse gas public inquiry and its recommendations cannot be understated. This organisation, during its short life of six years, sat at the pinnacle of Commonwealth government advisory bodies. Its voice on economic matters was authoritative. There was another Industry Commission inquiry underway at the same time, this one into the electricity and gas industries. Here is an important quote from the report of that inquiry:

> The efficient use of energy … requires governments to ensure that external costs, such as environmental damage, are included in supply decisions … impact(s) on the environment … derive from … the use of coal, gas or water to generate electricity.

And yet there is more worth quoting from that report where it dealt with greenhouse gas emissions:

> … approaches, such as transferable emission rights and pollution taxes, offer greater scope for achieving reduced environmental impact at minimum cost [however] … Not all of the environmental impacts associated with electricity and gas supply industries can be efficiently controlled through emission rights and taxes. Regulation may be the more efficient option when dealing with … extremely hazardous pollutants or where the metering of emissions is impossible, or very costly. However, attempts should be made to implement emission rights and tax schemes where environmental impacts are amenable to control through such measures … This will encourage energy utilities to adopt

> more environmentally friendly supply techniques and, through higher prices, also encourage consumers to conserve more energy.
>
> Industry Commission, 1991, p. 198

In 1992, the then Australian Environment Minister, Ros Kelly, and the Australian Ambassador for the Environment, Penny Wensley, went to the Earth Summit meeting in Rio. Overall, the outcomes of the Earth Summit were positive. Governments around the world became enthused to take positive action on environmental problems. It was agreed to establish the United Nations Framework Convention on Climate Change (UNFCCC). Two years after the Rio meeting this body came into effect.

By 1997, enough progress had been made to convince governments to design a formal protocol by which the industrialised economies would act to reduce greenhouse gas emissions. The agreement was named, as United Nations convention dictates, after the place where the delegates met. This happened to be Kyoto, Japan, hence the Kyoto Protocol.

Under the protocol, developing countries where not required to reduce emissions. Three rich countries came out of the Kyoto agreement with permission to increase emissions, while the rest agreed to reductions. Two of the three allowed to increase emissions, Iceland and Norway, where granted exclusion as their economies where based on non-polluting energy sources (respectively, geo-thermal and hydro-electricity). Australia was the third country excluded and got the best deal of all participating countries. This was negotiated by then Environment Minister, Robert Hill. Hill is a small "l" liberal with great intellect and commitment to environmentalism. Australia's deal was based on a reduction in land clearing and the regrowth of forests, with the trees taking in carbon dioxide

Notwithstanding this favourable outcome at the Kyoto meeting, John Howard as the then Prime Minister refused to ratify the Kyoto Protocol. The only other nation to reject what was truly a landmark treaty was the United States. Whether or not the United States requested Australia's support on this we don't know, but it would be consistent with realpolitik deal-making.

In 2007, the national government in Australia changed hands. The conservative government headed by Howard was beaten by the Labor Party with Kevin Rudd as Prime Minister. Rudd ratified the Kyoto Protocol and Australia's international status improved. In 2008, Rudd announced a "cap and trade" scheme. This meant imposing a limit on the emission of greenhouse gases by major industries. Permits to emit a set percentage of carbon dioxide were to be issued to the participating firms. These permits could be bought and sold. The theory behind the scheme was that businesses with the cleanest technology would purchase permits from the less clean businesses and the former would come to dominate their sectors. We were not to see this idea in operation in Australia.

Prime Minister Rudd did not control the Senate, Australia's upper house, and his scheme was destined to fail from lack of parliamentary support. Before that there came a glimmer of hope. In 2009, a potential saviour of the cap and trade scheme came along in the form of leader of the Liberal Party, Malcolm Turnbull, a firm believer in climate science. The proof of this, in addition to his public announcements at the time, is that he has covered the roof of his very large house in Sydney with solar panels plus has invested in significant battery storage.

Turnbull agreed that the Liberal Party would support the Rudd scheme in the Senate. This did not suit the then numerically strong conservative faction in his party. This group comprised so-called "climate-change deniers", anti-big-government ideologues, and United Nations (world government) haters. The conservatives' candidate Tony Abbott challenged Turnbull for leadership of the Liberal Party and won, by one vote. This was the end of hope for Rudd. His scheme did not get through the Senate. From then on nothing went well for Rudd.

Rudd was eventually challenged by Julia Gillard and she became Australia's first female Prime Minister. She won the next election and in 2011 introduced for debate in parliament a carbon tax. It came into effect on 1 July 2012. Notwithstanding Gillard's success, Kevin Rudd wanted his job back and played a destructive role in the media. When he had undermined Gillard and had enough colleagues supporting him, he challenged her and became Prime Minister again. He did not last long in the job as the Labor Party was beaten in the next election and Tony Abbott became Prime Minister. Before the carbon tax had a chance to illustrate how it could reduce greenhouse gases it was repealed by the Abbott-led government on 17 July 2014.

If these events featuring climate change politics were not enough to cause great uncertainty in the minds of potential investors in solar and other non-fossil fuel energy sources, there was yet another unusual deposing of a sitting Prime Minister. On the evening of 14 September 2015, Turnbull with the support of a majority of his party challenged and defeated Abbott and replaced him as Prime Minister. With the change of leadership of the Liberal Party there was an expectation that climate change policy would revert to an approach more sympathetic to clean energy.

Writing in August 2018, we witnessed yet another "political assassination". Prime Minister Malcolm Turnbull allowed a contest for the position of Prime Minister. He did not contest it. As events unfolded his challenger, Peter Dutton, spurred on by Tony Abbott and a host of media players of the same persuasion, failed to gain a majority of Liberal Party votes. Scott Morrison became the new Prime Minister. The "climate ("carbon" or "electricity") wars" had claimed another victim. And done considerable damage to Australia's self-image as a mature democracy.

Notwithstanding the existing situation where Australia's electricity policy is in limbo at Commonwealth level, there is value in understanding what the case was—and in practical terms remains. When eventually a new scheme is formulated, its architects will be forced to recognise the already obvious benefits of the citizen's solar revolution. Its viability is proof that a bottom up, financially-driven initiative is trumping an embarrassing political mess.

The previous government had a target of to reduce greenhouse gas emissions by 26 to 28 percent of the 2005 level by 2030. That government was confronted with an awkward decision, of its own making, to extend the renewable energy target (RET) as recommended in advice given to it by the head of an inquiry that the government established. This inquiry was asked to review energy and electricity policy and make recommendations as to future action. However, it was prohibited from considering either a carbon emissions tax or a cap and trade scheme. The inquiry's second-best option was to recommend an extension to the RET, something called a Clean Energy Target (CET). One of the things we learn in watching the "climate wars" play out is the symbolic importance of language. The word tax is not to be used. Apparently, a CET is not a RET in name.

Carbon taxes, cap and trade schemes and subsidies are not the only instruments that governments can use to limit and then reduce carbon dioxide being released into the atmosphere. Since 2001, the Commonwealth government has set mandatory targets for an increase in renewable electric energy, with the objective to reduce fossil-fuel based electricity generation. We have briefly discussed this before in the context of subsidising households and small businesses install solar panels, but here we shall give more attention to the concept. There are two schemes to increase the percentage of electricity generated by renewable sources, one for large-scale emitters of carbon dioxide such as power-houses (LRETs) and one for households and otherwise small generators and users of electricity (SRETs).

The schemes are based on two principles. One is a renewable energy target which in theory will become stricter and stricter as time goes by, with the aim of containing and then reducing the amount of carbon dioxide emitted in Australia. The other principle is the allocation by the government of "tradable certificates". These are assigned to generators of electricity for each megawatt hour of renewable power they generate. We have discussed these in relation to households and other small electricity users.

The certificates can be bought and sold. As a consequence of renewable energy becoming an ever-greater proportion of the total electricity output, the less efficient coal-fired generators are destined to close down. Their age is a major factor. By this process the renewable electricity producers will come to generate more of the total. The amount of greenhouse gases released per unit of electricity generated will decrease. This process is to continue until the goal set for renewable electricity is achieved. Of course, what that goal is set at is the most important feature of the scheme. As an aside it is worth noting that the tradable certificate concept has the benefit of being accepted by economic purists because it is viewed as relying on "market principles".

At present, the scheme for the large-scale generators requires that 33,000 Gigawatt-hours (GWh) of electricity has to come from renewables by 2020. It should be noted that this is a significant reduction from the 41,000 GWh that was the requirement until the change of Commonwealth government policy in June 2015. The change had the potential to put a damper on investment in large-scale renewable projects. However, the decreasing coast of solar and wind electricity technologies has compensated for this change and investment has increased substantially.

An electricity producer, say one based around electricity generated from coal, needs a certain number of certificates to meet the renewable electricity target. If not meeting the target, the coal producer purchases certificates from business operators who have acquired certificates from those who have added to the total of renewable electricity. The certificates are then surrendered to the Commonwealth government. The scheme is a little more complicated than this, but that need not bother us. If you have been through the situation of installing solar panels, you will be familiar with the process for the small-scale RET scheme.

Some commentators assert that the RET scheme, which works as an incentive to households purchasing renewable energy systems is a significant cost to those householders who do not install roof-top panels. The Australian Energy Market Operator (AEMO) has studied this matter and found the cost to be relatively minor, on average 5 per cent increase on bills across the nation.

In addition to the Commonwealth emissions target (the national target), the Australian States and Territories have set their own renewable energy targets, some far more ambitious than the Commonwealth target. While this is to be welcomed, the range of schemes and the fact that targets tend to change with a change of government does not lead to the certainty that is much prized by investors. Renewable energy targets are not set in stone. Of course, how to achieve that in a democracy is not obvious.

There is the other key part of Australia's journey to a renewable electricity future, feed-in tariffs. We have noted that feed-in tariffs where instrumental in kick-starting the roll-out of photovoltaic panels on the roofs of residences and small business establishments. Their excess electricity is fed into the nearby grid. Solar and wind farms also feed the electricity they produce into a grid (unless they are installed by businesses capable of using all the electricity produced). In their case commercial-in-confidence arrangements are made between the operator of the farms and the operator of the grid. Our attention here is to elaborate on our earlier discussion on household feed-in tariffs.

The commencement of this approach was in 2008, when the Council of Australian Governments issued "National Principles for Feed-in Tariff Schemes". Some jurisdictions commenced by offering high feed-in rates on a "net" basis; however, in the early days there were some "gross" schemes. Under the net schemes a householder is paid only for the electricity in excess of the household's needs. The excess is what is fed into a grid. On the other hand, a gross tariff means the householder is paid for the total amount of electricity generated by its panels. Who gets to use the electricity is irrelevant.

It warrants noting in passing that Germany introduced a gross feed-in tariff scheme in 1991. The nature of the German scheme and its very early start date explains why that country became a leader in renewable electricity technology.

The Victorian tariff rate from November 2009 to December 2011 was 60 cents/kWh. A household could have no more than 5 kW installed capacity. The Queensland scheme, also limited to 5 kW, was 44 cents/kWh from 2008, but with tariff reductions made by the Queensland government over the following years only a fortunate few have retained the 44 cents/kWh tariff. Different tariffs were set by the different governments, and in due course lowered. We have noted above that recently electricity retailers have increased the feed-in tariffs they offer. The ever-changing feed-in tariffs and retail discounts, plus the differences across jurisdictions render providing advice to those contemplating installing solar panels—except on an individual basis—not recommended.

Notwithstanding the success of the household feed-in tariff schemes, the rapid increase in solar and wind farms, and the likelihood that the national renewable electricity target will be met, what we have is a smorgasbord of policies that limit the progress possible. The higgly-piggly chopping and changing, according to ideological viewpoints is not good public policy, from both economic and environmental perspectives.

Paul Syvret (*Courier Mail*, 11/2/2017) described the nation's electricity policy as follows:

> It is a dog's breakfast in which private investors lack policy clarity (who would commit billions to a new base load coal-fired power station amid the

> current uncertainty?) and governments wrestle with balancing the workings of the free market and the longer-term strategic planning and the demands of both voters and industry thoroughly jacked off by rising electricity prices.

Syvret concludes by suggesting that the solution rests with government control of electricity production and distribution rather than the miss-mash of private and public participants that we have today, with their differing agendas and incentives. It would need to be the national government that takes control unless policies were in harmony across all jurisdictions.

Syvret is not the only person to address the barriers and challenges of a renewal-energy future for Australia. Colleagues at the University of Queensland (Byrnes et. al., 2013) comment:

> Significant policy barriers still exist at the federal and state levels … which have reduced the effectiveness of a concerted national effort to deploy renewables. [They conclude:] the reality for any government in attempting to capture all external costs and to address non-market failures is limited by political considerations, institutional experience, and the perceived need to make trade-offs between affordability, jobs, and existing industries.

Five years later the same sentiment remains applicable. While the technical matters that we have discussed need to be addressed and be resolved on scientific and economic grounds, the political and institutional factors that Syvret and others bring to the table are fundamental and, given political posturing and intransigence, more difficult to resolve. A spokesperson for BHP, a company that spends $300 million annually on power, is reported saying that Australia's commitment to addressing climate change has been "inconsistent and lacking in direction", and a spokesperson for GE said that Australia needed "a national energy blueprint" to set policies "well beyond election cycles". These comments were made to journalists writing in the *Weekend Australian* of 18–19 March 2017. One of the articles was headed "Companies Lash Lack of Clear Policy". Syvret had an industry executive tell him: "We don't know what the … rules will be next week, let alone in 10 years, and that makes it nearly impossible to make investment decisions".

As we write, the present Commonwealth government has just scrapped what was called the National Energy Guarantee (NEG). All States and Territories were required to support the scheme if it was to come into practice. That was challenge number one. The second challenge was that the legislation to establish it had to be passed by the Senate, where the government did not, and does not, have a majority of votes. The third challenge was for the then Prime Minister, Malcolm Turnbull, to have majority support for the scheme within the Liberal Party. It is not known if he did have sufficient support as he volunteered to walk away from a party embroiled in internecine conflict. The new Prime Minister wasted no time in killing off the NEG.

A body known as the Energy Security Board (ESB) had modelled the impact of the NEG and found that it would meet the government's commitment to have greenhouse gas emissions at 26 per cent below 2005 levels by 2030. This body had informed householders that on average they would save $550 per year on electricity bills. This, obviously very welcome, outcome was according to the ESB, in the main, the result of a massive pipeline of renewable electricity projects coming online in 2020–21. A figure of 7,800 MW is reported to be in the pipeline—very exciting.

With the Commonwealth government's decision to walk away from the NEG, we are back to where we were 10 years ago on electricity policy. Once again we are being forced to start from scratch by our Commonwealth politicians. How many failed attempts have there been! Yet, regardless of what they do or don't do, the sun has kept on rising every morning, and the renewable energy pipeline is not choked and, hence, will deliver a very large addition of solar and wind power.

The success of the solar revolution is getting closer by the day.

SECTION II

Australia's Potential: Making Economic Sense

4.

Abundant Sunshine and Falling Water

KEELEY HARTZER AND TOR HUNDLOE

The renewable electricity revolution in Australia has been driven by the nation's citizens installing roof top solar panels. This revolution commenced slowly in 2008 and then accelerated. In the past two years, home-owners have been joined by investors in both solar and wind farms. Notwithstanding the stale-mated "electricity wars", investors have recognised the potential—it could be said that they have seen the future and they are it. Before the start of the solar revolution, the only significant amount of renewable electricity was derived from hydro-electric schemes such as the famous Snowy Mountains and the Tasmanian ones.

The potential for solar-derived electricity in Australia is, and not to over-state it, enormous. In 2014, the organisations Geoscience and BREE estimated that the unharvested solar energy in close-to-grid and flat locations in Australia is in the order of 500 times the annual energy consumption in Australia. Worth reading again.

To make clear our potential to harness immense amounts of solar electricity, we start by noting that of all continents, Australia has the highest incident solar energy per unit of land. A CSIRO scientist, Wes Stein, has calculated that a solar farm of 50 square kilometres could meet all of Australia's electricity needs. On this basis, we are undoubtedly a lucky country! Figure 4 shows on a global scale the areas of high solar radiation. Australia is the only industrialised country blessed with an overall high level.

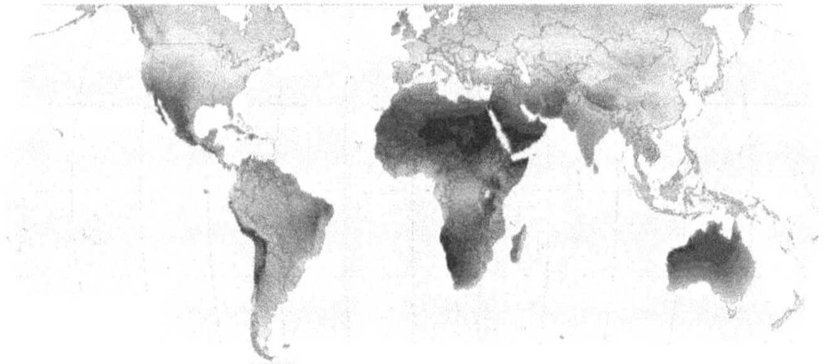

Figure 4. Global Horizontal Irradiation: dark is highest: Source: SolarGIS

Going east to west the width of Australia means that there is approximately three hour's difference from when the sun rises in the east to when it sets in the west. This measurement is based on official times in Brisbane and Perth, not actual sunrise-sunset difference on any day of the year. North to south, there are the year-round, short sunlit days near the Equator (such as in Darwin); and in summer, down south early sunrises and drawn-out twilights, while winter has much shorter sunlit days. In mid-summer, there are in the order of 15 hours of sunlight in Melbourne, while there are only 12.5 hours in Darwin, and for the latter city this is a year-long constant.

Lygon Street in Melbourne is an open-air, footpath-based, sunlit dining precinct until 9 pm in summer, whereas darkness would have engulfed Darwin before 7 pm.

This geographical spread extends by many hours the sunlight available to be harvested across Australia if only an extensive, nation-wide grid existed. One can imagine an electricity grid criss-crossing the nation, generating solar electricity on the east coast at Byron Bay from 7 o'clock in the morning until 6 o'clock in the evening; at 9 o'clock in the morning eastern time we are in the "Red Centre" (around Alice Springs) for the commencement of its day where huge photovoltaic solar farms (and in years to come solar thermal farms) kick in; next before noon eastern time, solar farms at Shark Bay on the west coast commence generating electricity. By the time that the sun's power on the west coast has lost its intensity at 6 pm western time it is already 9 pm of a night on the east coast. This range of available sunlight makes the proposition of a truly national grid with adequate storage, and feed-in solar electricity a serious proposition, the cost of a new grid notwithstanding. We would add in wind-generated electricity to be fed in to this "super grid". Storage would be a mix of very large batteries and pumped-storage hydro-electricity in the mountainous coastal areas.

Moving electricity very long distances does result in some loss, yet the grid that runs from far-north Queensland to Melbourne with the undersea connection to Tasmania, and a link west to Adelaide and Port Lincoln, suggests that the losses are not high and long-range networks are economically and technologically feasible.

We have noted that wind-generated electricity is a necessary complement to solar power. This source of electricity is competitive on price with fossil fuel-derived electricity and is has developed at a quicker pace than solar farms in the past. There are wind farms along the southern coast of Australia, from Albany across the Great Australian Bight into coastal Victoria and Tasmania's north-west coast. And we must not overlook locations somewhat distant from the coast where there are highland windy areas suitable for wind farms, such as the New England tableland and south-east Queensland. As we write, the largest wind farm to be built in Australia is under construction in the latter area. The advantage of wind farms, over and above the fact that they provide cheaper electricity than coal or gas, is that they can co-exist with many types of farming. Wind farms have tiny footprints compared to all other sources of electricity, including gas and coal.

There are three ways by which Australia will come to have a renewable-powered electricity system. One is the super grid concept discussed above. Another is a decentralised system based on stand-alone, off-grid community systems. Some of these already exist in remote parts of the nation. Towns of some size could obtain their electricity from a nearby solar farm working in combination with a wind farm (or farms), and if the water resources exist nearby a pumped-storage hydro-electricity generator. This arrangement would take some of the pressure off upgrading and extending the existing grids.

However, we don't anticipate decentralising the massive east coast grid. Could it be extended? Maybe a super grid is not needed, regardless of whether or not it is technologically feasible or economic. The third option is the most likely for the present: it is to work with the existing grids, constructing solar and wind farms on suitable land in close proximity to these grids. This is what is occurring now. The utility-scale solar and wind farms that have been constructed recently are in near-to-a-grid places like Clare outside of Home Hill in Queensland. The area is average cattle grazing country. On a sheep station near Port Augusta in South Australia a solar thermal power station is planned. Renewable electricity developments are not taking farm land of high value.

Before dismissing the rather utopian vision of the super grid, let us consider what would be required. Significant advances in transmission technology would be essential. First, transmission losses would have to be minimised. Second and most importantly, there would have to be a seamless integration of intermittent electricity generation of solar and wind with 24/7 hydro-power, and for the next 10 years or thereabouts integration with coal and gas-fired electricity. Maybe the sensible decision is to forget the interesting idea of a super grid.

Turning to something more practical and of immediate need, pumped storage hydro-electricity. We have discussed this technology in some length already, however we believe it needs further analysis. It has been the "sleeper" in dealing with intermittency in electricity supply in the new world of renewables. The conventional wisdom that all Australian rivers of any consequence have been tapped for their conventional hydro-electric potential is true, but this is only true if hydro-electricity is only viewed as a one-way, downhill use of gravity to power a turbine at the bottom of a reservoir. As noted earlier, Australia's electricity engineers have neglected pumped-storage hydro, the major exception being the "Tumut 3 Power Station" at Talbingo in the Snowy Mountains. We have been somewhat of a laggard on this matter because it has not been needed in a coal-rich country.

With the rapid increase in solar and wind electricity and the intermittency issues that are arising we will not be able to afford this neglect. It is not that the concept of pumped-storage is new; for some considerable time, pumped-storage hydro-electricity has played a significant role in a number of countries, such as in the mountainous parts of Italy, France and Germany but mainly in the United States, China and Japan.

Pumped-storage hydro-electricity is based on pairs of reservoirs at different altitudes. Water from the higher reservoir is released to fall and do its work at the bottom of the fall in turning turbines to produce electricity. Having performed this function it is gathered in the lower reservoir from which it is pumped back to the higher one, to fall again to once more generate electricity, and so on. The electricity needed to pump the water uphill would ideally be sourced from solar farms in the middle of the day when much electricity is produced. Simple, but brilliant!

It is the cheapest form of storing electricity, acting like a mammoth battery but with a much longer life span which makes it economically attractive. A battery might last for 25 years, while a pumped-storage hydro-electric turbine has three times that life and the reservoir has a minimum life of 100 years. There are minor downsides. Evaporation depletes the stored water. There are also losses in the conversion into electricity. Combined these two negative forces result in a 70 to 80 per cent efficiency. But to solve the intermittency problem in creating a seamless co-ordination of heterogeneous electricity generators, as we have today with solar, wind, hydro-electricity, coal and gas there is no better solution on economic and environmental grounds, than pumped storage hydro-electricity. No doubt those who despise hydro-electricity will find cause/s to disagree. Already they are running a pseudo-environmental campaign that endangered and threatened animal species might trump Snowy 2.0. If that were to occur, it would be a miscarriage of rational decision-making.

The search for appropriate Australian pumped-hydro sites was undertaken recently. We have mentioned the exciting results. They proved to be beyond anyone's expectation. Andrew Blakers and his colleagues from the Australian National University, funded by ARENA, released their findings on 21 September 2017. They identified an enormous number of appropriate sites across Australia. If Andrew Blakers, a professor of engineering, has anything to do with it, off-river, closed loop pumped-storage electricity will provide virtually all the power needed to aid solar and wind electricity providers when Mother Nature restricts their operation. Professor Blakers and his team have identified 22,000 possible sites (far, far more than needed), the vast majority of them in the hills running all the way down Australia's east coast into Tasmania and across to

South Australia. Western Australia and the Northern Territory also have their share. Only a tiny proportion of the suitable sites, about 22 (or 3,600 hectares), are required to meet the nation's demand. Rather small reservoirs, of between 10 to 100 hectares, need to be built. At the smaller scale this is equivalent to building farm dams. One of a pair of the dams would be at a high elevation of 300 metres or more above the lower dam. This altitude difference is what is known as the "head". The loss of efficiency in the loop from top-to-bottom-to top is not large, as wc havc pointed out.

There is a potential political problem in developing pumped-storage hydro-electricity.

Attempt to get approval to build a large dam on a river in Australia and contemplate rejection. Build a few small dams away from National Parks and other valuable sites, in steep hilly country where agriculture production is not lost and be in an uncertain world. It might go well, particularly if promoted as an essential component of bringing about carbon-free electricity. The again, it might not.

Most good sites are away from rivers and none are in National Parks or urban areas. As a consequence, land use conflicts should not arise. We say "should not" as it is difficult to predict if, and when, a genuine objection, or a not-in-my-backyard (NIMBY) one, will be lodged. Blakers and his team reported: "We found so many good potential sites that only the best 0.1 per cent will be needed". Converted to numbers that is 22 pumped-hydro-electric sites across Australia with the ability to support a 100 per cent renewable electricity system.

We have discussed battery storage previously, but it is important not to overlook the potential for vastly improved and potentially inexpensive battery storage as a means to overcome intermittency. The battery industry argues that prices are falling and investing in batteries makes economic sense. At household level inexpensive batteries would allow households to go off-grid. The proof will be evident when a significant number of householder's purchase batteries; and at utility level if giant batteries can compete on price with pumped-storage. The South Australian government has had a large battery since late 2017. However, the question that needs to be answered by a thorough cost-benefit analysis is: at utility scale does pumped-storage hydro-electricity trump battery storage in cost?

Australia is moving into the most significant change in electricity generation and distribution since the time when the first small power stations were built in the suburbs of our major cities, and that was more than one hundred years ago. The change is being driven by two forces. One is easily recognised, the need to address climate change through the reduction, and eventual elimination, of fossil-fuel fired electricity generation. The other is not as well recognised. It is the dramatic reduction in the cost of renewable sources and both households and investors reacting to this with unexpected enthusiasm. As we have argued above, as solar and wind generated electricity expand, the importance of addressing climate change is likely to take a back seat to the financial benefits of renewable electricity. "No regrets" is always a winner.

With the above necessary digression completed, we can return to outline the immense potential Australia has to generate solar electricity. The solar radiation falling on Australia in any year is more than 10,000 times the nation's annual energy consumption according to the experts in Geoscience Australia. It has been estimated that a relatively small area of sun-drenched central Australia would, if converted into a very large solar farm (more likely, a number of smaller solar farms), harvest all the sun's energy we need to supply the nation's electricity. In fact, it is argued that Australia's desert centre could be the site of solar farms producing enough electricity for the world. We note this to illustrate how much sunlight we have. We are not utopian.

Various studies have suggested how much desert land in high insolation regions is required to produce all the world's electricity. An example is the estimate by Seifried and Witzel (2010, p. 26): "an area of the Sahara 200 km by 200 km—roughly the size of Kentucky or twice the size of Wales—would suffice to cover the current global energy consumption". These authors admit that this might be expecting too much in terms of efficiency and suggest that at quite low levels of efficiency the area needed would be no more than 700 km by 700 km to meet global energy demand. Figure 5 shows the extent of this area relative to Africa. If the task of producing the global population's demand for electricity was assigned to Australia rather than Africa, the area of land required is shown in Figure 5. This 49,000 square kilometre area is a not much more than double the world's largest cattle station, Anna Creek, which also is in Australia, in desert country near the South Australia-Queensland border.

Figure 5. Areas Needed to Produce All the World's Electricity. Source: Based on Solar GIS

What is technically possible, as with the Sahara Desert providing electricity for a large proportion of the human population, is at the time of writing, both economically and politically out of the question. We would write in the same vein about the likelihood of Australia's very extensive deserts playing anything but a regional role in the export of solar-generated electricity. However, in a future chapter we ask that thought be given to the export of solar electricity to our neighbours. On various grounds it might not be a bad idea.

The best idea to have been acted on recently is the massive pumped-storage hydro-electricity project known as Snowy 2.0. Not all policy-making has been a dud. History books will contain a new chapter on the already iconic Snowy Mountains Hydro-Electric Scheme. And the history books will record the name of the nation-building Prime Minister who promoted this initiative, Malcolm Turnbull, when most others from his era are forgotten. Some wins are more important than others.

5.

Sunny Days in the Outback

KEELEY HARTZER AND TOR HUNDLOE

In this this chapter we focus on solar farms. Our focus is on photovoltaic solar farms, as other than small demonstration and experimental solar thermal plants, none are in operation in Australia. This is not to overlook significant potential for solar thermal farms.

To illustrate the very dramatic increase in constructing photovoltaic solar farms consider these numbers. In 2016, 125 MW capacity was brought on line. In 2017, large solar projects with a capacity of over 2000 MW were under or near construction. This represents more than a 12-fold increase. A significant proportion of this increased capacity is still under construction as of writing this book. We don't expect all these farms to be putting electricity into the grid as some will direct their power to their business, dodging the middle man.

We have already made reference to the world's longest interconnected electricity grid. It serves the majority of Australia's population, industry and commerce. While that is most welcome, this area is but a slither of the vast Australian continent. Not many other countries face the challenge of providing electricity to a few people and industries in far-flung parts of the country. Yet, a demographic and geographical study results in a rather impressive list of developed countries with skewed populations as is the Australian case. They include Russia, Canada, Norway, Finland, Sweden and New Zealand. If Scotland was a country it could be included. Providing electricity to large countries with remote communities is an economic and, partly, technological challenge.

In Australia there are many remote communities, small towns and very large outback pastoral properties that are not connected to a grid, or a low voltage "single-wire earth return" (SWER) transmission line extending from a grid. The latter are low voltage transmission lines that use the earth as the return path for the current, hence avoiding the need for a second (neutral) wire.

Most remote communities, small towns and pastoral stations obtain their electricity from diesel generators. A few have hybrid systems combining diesel generation with very small solar farms, and there are a small number reliant on gas. These isolated electricity consumers include over 1,000 Indigenous communities (mainly in the Northern Territory and Western Australia). Some of these have very small resident populations. There are other electricity solutions for remote communities. For example, wind power complements diesel power on Thursday Island. Thargomindah is the only community to have geothermal-hydro power. As we write there are research projects underway into the feasibility of providing electricity by modern geothermal-hydro plants in other Queensland western towns, such as Winton, Quilpie, Normanton and Longreach.

If we focus on communities and towns with a population of 50 plus people, there are in total 192 towns and aboriginal communities throughout Australia that are not connected to any grid network. The vast majority (148) rely on diesel-generated electricity, while 32 have diesel generators coupled with one or more of gas, solar, hydro, wind or geothermal electricity generation. Eight communities are serviced by gas alone; two rely solely on wind-power; and one solely on hydro-electricity and another on liquefied natural gas.

The Northern Territory (NT) has a small grid network and distribution system which runs around the top of the Territory. There are also smaller grids in the Tennant Creek area and Alice Springs area. Most of the tiny towns near to these two centres obtain electricity from local networks. However, there are 68 towns in the NT which are too far away from a network to be connected. Most of these towns are Indigenous communities with low population numbers.

There is another remote area of the nation that is also too far from a grid and requires each community to have its own electricity supply. The Torres Strait with a total of 21 towns or villages spread over a series of isolated islands is solely reliant on diesel generation, except for the contribution made by the wind turbines on Thursday Island. The rest of Queensland has 27 towns and communities which are not on a grid; these towns are in the western-most and the far northern areas.

Interestingly, there are two island communities that are very close to the main grid running down the Queensland east coast but are not connected to it. One is the Palm Island community, off-shore but close to Townsville; the other is a private resort called Couran Cove on South Stradbroke Island, again very close to the mainland. This island is a part of the City of the Gold Coast. It proved cheaper for the resort owner to install his own generator than link to the grid.

The bottom of eastern South Australia as far west as Port Lincoln is connected to the east coast grid, whereas towns in the north of the State such as Cooper Pedy have their own stand-alone electricity systems. In Tasmania, the two islands located at its top (in Bass Strait) are not connected to a grid network; however, it is planned to connect them sometime in the future.

Progress is being made in bringing solar electricity to the nation's remote communities, yet there is still much to do. The first high profile project in a remote town proved to be very disappointing and as a consequence slowed down interest in replacing diesel generators with solar power. Because we aim to present warts and all assessment of solar electricity, we discuss this case. The fact that former Prime Minister Kevin Rudd and former Queensland Premier Anna Blyth are the lead actors suggests its prominence at the time. This experimental solar electricity project enticed these two to travel to tiny outback town to attend its opening.

Some geography is necessary to set the scene. No electricity grid extends into the dark-coloured area in Figure 6. This is where diesel generators are used; if not diesel, there are a few hybrid systems of solar and diesel or other combinations, and a wind turbine on Thursday Island.

Figure 6. The East Coast Grid in Queensland: white shading. Source: Based on Ergon Energy

Most remote Australian communities are Indigenous settlements. A minority are small townships catering for the needs of the local graziers. Scattered throughout remote Australia Aboriginal and Torres Islander communities, the Indigenous population living in these communities is in the order of 80,000. One third of these communities are very small, with populations under 200 people.

In terms of access to a major electricity grid, the percentage of the remote Indigenous population is a meagre 28%. Of the remainder, 62% obtain their electricity from a community diesel, or diesel-hybrid generator. Solar hybrid installations are only a very small percentage of the total. Yet, these communities are in areas of very high solar radiation, with very few days of cloud and rain; and their land has little agricultural use making covering small amounts of it with solar panels costless in terms of foregone agricultural productivity.

There is the price of diesel to take into account, the cost of repairs and maintenance of the generators, and the substantial cost of transporting diesel very long distances. Electricity is dear in these remote communities. It makes no difference, except to the residents, that it is subsidised.

To give an indication of the amount of diesel used in remote area generators, the Power and Water Corporation in the Northern Territory reported that 30 million litres of diesel was used in the Territory in 2012. At the cost of $1.50/ litre this amounts to $45 million per year. The situation on a State/Territory basis differs; for example, there are no remote communities in Victoria while there are many in the Northern Territory and Western Australia but in these jurisdictions, there are very few remote towns of any size. Queensland is different again, with small towns stretching to its distant borders and it has a host of small island communities in the Torres Strait.

In Queensland there are 33 remote (called "isolated" in Queensland) towns and communities not connected to a major grid. Diesel electricity generation is a component, in the great majority of cases the only component, of the electricity for these towns and communities. Four Queensland towns/communities have hybrid systems, Thursday Island, Birdsville, Windorah and Doomadgee. The hybrid systems are in a sense experimental in that their cost and performance are monitored, and the results have an impact on future decisions regarding electricity supply to isolated areas.

Some systems are more novel than others. The Windorah system was the first in Queensland and was at the experimental end of the scale, in as much it relies on concentrated photovoltaic dishes, each containing 112 mirrors, rather than the common flat panels. It marries solar-generated electricity with diesel-generated electricity. The trials and tribulations of this experiment are likely to be of historical interest.

It will help comprehension if the town of Windorah is put into demographic and geographical perspective. Windorah is a town of approximately 100 people. The photograph of its main street is a story in one frame (see Figure 7). One does not know the Australian outback if not having driven a Holden "ute"—these days more likely a Toyota Hilux—down the main street of a town like Windorah. Nearby towns are smaller and their main streets wider, as if in fear of traffic jams. These towns are Jundah, Stonehenge and Yaraka, the latter's population can be counted on two hands. These tiny towns are all situated in the Barcoo Shire, a Queensland local government district.

Figure 7. The Main Street of Windorah. Photo: Steven Robert Bowden

The Barcoo Shire is mainly cattle grazing country, previously sheep and cattle. The graziers' favourite grass, Mitchell grass, is abundant in good seasons. As Figure 6 shows, Windorah is beyond any SWER line, meaning it is not connected to the main grid running north-south through Queensland. We would find no linesman travelling that far west looking for faults to repair, however outback towns a little east of Windorah would have the benefit of a Queensland equivalent to the "Wichita Lineman" singing as he journeyed:

I am a lineman of the county,
And I drive the main road,
Searching in the sun
For another overload.

With thanks to song writer Jimmy Webb
and singer Glen Campbell

Windorah is approximately 1,200 km from Brisbane and over 300 km from the much larger outback town of Longreach. Windorah has an airstrip and hence can be accessed by commercial flights, a matter of some importance when the formal "opening" of its solar farm took place. For a small town it has a wide range of commercial and recreational services, however this is to be expected, and necessary, in remote outback towns. There is a general store which as well as selling groceries provides take-away snacks. There is, naturally, a hotel and it has an enviable reputation. Accommodation for travellers is available in the motel section as well as in a caravan park. As one would expect, there is a service station, a post office, a primary health care centre, a library, council depot, fire station, shire hall and an information centre-cum-museum. There is an arts and craft shop and, because this is where horse-power sufficed until recently, a racecourse. So much for such a small country town.

Until late in 2008, Windorah's residents and small businesses relied on electricity generated by diesel fuel. Leading up to 2008, someone with the power to do these things decided to undertake an exciting experiment. This person noticed that the town experienced on average 200 days of the year when there were seven to eight hours of sunlight, the skies were clear of cloud. The rest of the year also got plenty of sunshine. It does not rain much in Australia's outback.

The decision was made to spend $4.5 million in installing a small solar farm on the outskirts of the town. The project was politically very significant. This was at the very beginning of the solar electricity revolution. The political significance was such that it drew the then Prime Minister and Queensland Premier to the town to launch a tiny small solar farm in a town most Australians could not place on a map. The opening was on 14 December 2008.

Today one would expect an order of magnitude or more of taxpayers' money (let us say, $4.5 billion) to be involved to have both a Prime Minister and Premier venture far into the outback for the equivalent of a sod-turning ceremony. In 2008, the experiment was a minor historical event, and this makes its success or failure important. At the time of the opening of the solar farm, Australian politics was very much focussed on how to reduce greenhouse gases. Climate change and how Australia was to deal with it dominated politics. Anything to illustrate that there were practical alternatives to coal, gas or diesel-fired electricity generation warranted promotion—if you were on that side of the argument.

The official announcements at the opening of the solar farm were optimistic to the extreme. The Queensland Premier at the time, Anna Bligh stated:

> It's an exciting day for Queensland, as Premier I want us to move from being the sunshine state of Australia to the solar state of Australia.
>
> ABC News, 14/12/2008

The Premier went on to say that Windorah would be "the first town to be fully solar powered". What she meant by this is not known, as the solar farm was not able to supply electricity for 24 hours per day for 365 days per year. It was a hybrid system relying on diesel generation when electricity demand exceeded what the sun could supply. It did have the capacity to provide electricity to the 60 houses and business in Windorah on sunny days. This would meet the town's needs if the electricity was not intermittent as solar electricity is.

The Windorah solar farm consists of five concentrated reflectors (dishes). This makes it different to a regular photovoltaic solar farm. The dishes were reported as being 35 per cent efficient, which is a good result. Achieving this was a considerable advance in technology. Not that far back, in the early 1990s, 15 per cent efficiency was the standard, as the Industry Commission noted in 1991. The dishes sit on masts, and are aligned north-south, rotating 360 degrees, following the sun. Various commentators have likened them to sun flowers.

We now come to the claims that were made for the Windorah solar farm. It was supposed to provide between 100,000 and 360,000 kilowatts/hour of electricity, or average 180,000 kilowatts of electricity for 10 months of the year. In achieving this target, the solar farm was to save 100,000 litres of diesel per year. If the cost of diesel is $1.50/litre, the saving would be $150,000 per year. If we assume for illustrative purposes that the life of the solar farm is 30 years, it would pay for itself in saved diesel costs: 30 years at $150,000/year = $4.5 million. The reduced cost is one part of a two-part justification for the expenditure of $4.5 million. The other part was its reduction in greenhouse gas emissions. If the solar farm proved successful it could be replaced at the end of its life and the savings of diesel fuel and reduction in emissions continue indefinitely.

Based on the simple arithmetic used above, we could claim the investment in the solar farm was justified. Many old-style economists would not be satisfied with this simple calculation as they would wish to discount future benefits and costs. However, the economics of climate change has rendered the imposition of discount rates, except for tiny ones, obsolete economics. For a thorough explanation and analysis of this matter the reference is "The Stern Report".

After the solar farm was formally opened nothing was heard of it until a not too many years later when there emerged concerns as to its reliability. A hardly noticed comment by the electricity generator, Ergon Energy, took those who heard it by surprise. A report by ABC News on 30 May 2013, more than five years after the opening of the solar farm, carried a report by Ergon Energy spokesman, Bob Pleash: "there are no plans at this stage to construct more solar farms". Why? Had something gone wrong at Windorah?

Yes, apparently something had. Pleash explained that there had been problems with dust and birds impacting the photovoltaic dishes. These were the only excuses he gave for the curtailment of what was expected to be an ongoing roll-out of solar farms in remote areas of Queensland. Of the two problems he identified, dust should have been on Ergon Energy's radar as a potential problem from the onset.

Anyone who was contemplated building solar farms in desert environments would surely have addressed the matter of keeping the dishes clean during sand and dust storms. Such storms in Australia are not severe (not like the biting sand storms of the Sahara Desert) but they can carry large amounts of fine soil particles a long distance. Red outback Australian soils can be found in the snow-covered mountains of New Zealand. One would certainly expect some dust to settle on the solar dishes at Windorah.

For a very small-scale solar instalment such as the Windorah one, the dust problem could have been dealt with by employing a local person to clean the dishes when this was necessary. Dust storms, assuming that they are the major problem are infrequent and can be forecast and when they occur the results are observable, therefore subject to immediate action.

The other problem apparently was an occasional bird strike. This is more of puzzle, not that such could not be anticipated. Occasionally, birds crash into city building windows, house windows, car and truck windscreens and very infrequently are a serious problem for aircraft. We have learned to deal with bird strikes in these situations. A small solar farm should be no different.

It appears from additional statements by Bob Pleash, that the cost of installing the solar farm was decisive in the decision to curtail building more similar solar farms. The same ABC News broadcast reported him saying:

> In the current climate, whilst it is all well and good from an environmental point of view, Ergon's focus is very much about driving on affordability.

We get no insight to what "the current climate" refers to. An obvious guess is the "economic climate" in the State of Queensland. This is not the place to argue the strength of the Queensland, or Australian, economy but it would be remiss of us to not mention that on a global scale they have proven to be among the most resilient, healthy economies over the past three decades. Was the under-performance of the hybrid system the issue?

Had the solar farm performed as the Queensland Premier was told it would, it was affordable, as the analysis above illustrates. For reasons, not completely clear (dust and bird strikes noted), Ergon Energy admitted in the *Brisbane Times* of 24 August 2016 that from the beginning of 2009 to mid-2016, the solar farm had generated only 942,000 kilowatts of power, or about one third of what it was supposed to provide. And to make matters worse only 250,000 litres of diesel have been saved. If the savings are calculated on the basis of $1.50 litre, as previously, this amounts to $375,000; where had the solar farm operated at its expected level the saving would have been $1.2 million over that period. If this serious under-performance continued one can understand why the solar farm was not going to break even over its life span. Dust and bird strikes do not explain this poor performance. It remains unresolved; or if resolved, unreported.

There is another fundamental issue involved in analysing the success or otherwise of the solar farm. The simple financial case which we have put is only part of the story. Solar electricity generation is about reducing the emission of greenhouse gases. The Queensland Premier and the Prime Minister were hi-lighting it in travelling to distant Windorah to open the installation.

Diesel generators running on fossil fuel, as they do, emit greenhouse gases, while a solar farm does not, putting aside the matter of greenhouse gas emissions in the manufacture of solar dishes, plus emissions in transport and construction. While accepting that life-cycle emissions, which would account for these pre-installation carbon releases, are the ultimate measure, we can exclude them for present purposes. There are greenhouse gas emissions in building and installing diesel generators.

What is required to undertake a full economic analysis is to include the monetary benefits of reducing greenhouse gases. Given the sub-optimal performance over the past years only 250,000 litres of diesel have been saved. If there was no improvement in the operational efficiency of the solar farm, the total saving of diesel would amount to approximately only 940,000 litres of diesel over 30 years. This would result in the order of 2,600 tonnes of carbon dioxide saved. Any reduction of carbon dioxide, no matter how small, is considered a good thing in the context of limiting greenhouse impacts. But this experiment failed to deliver.

There is no accurate means of estimating the damage avoided by reducing emissions of carbon dioxide. To leave unrecognised and unreported the small amount of damage avoided by the operation of the Windorah solar farm would disappoint some readers. One, and it is only one, proxy measure of the benefit of not using the diesel fuel is the value of the carbon tax that was to apply in Australia at that time. It was $23 per tonne of carbon dioxide. For our purpose, we will use $25/tonne. If 2,600 tonnes are avoided, the sum is approximately $65,000. Admittedly, this is a very small amount. As the years pass by and greenhouse gases accumulate each tonne of carbon dioxide avoided will become more and more valuable. A price of $25/tonne could be a very serious underestimate in 20 to 30 years tine. Had the solar farm met its promise the savings in carbon dioxide emissions would have been near to 8,000 tonnes, valued at $200,000.

The Windorah solar farm was established as an experiment. To try things out and learn from success or failure is the reason to run experiments. This is done in laboratories 365 days of the year, year-in, year-out. Experiments in the field (the real world) are the ultimate proving ground. As the first of the hybrid solar-diesel systems using concentrating solar dishes, located in the outback where it is not uncommon for dust storms in periods of extended droughts, the need to keep the dishes clean is a major lesson. Considerable technological advances in system design, resulting in improved and less costly dishes, have occurred since the Windorah solar farm commenced operating at the beginning of 2009. With the improved technology solar farms such as the Windorah farm should be viable propositions.

However, there were other solar-based options available to Ergon Energy when it installed the concentrated solar dishes at Windorah. As we are not privy to the decision-making undertaken, we are not in a position to comment other than present an example of an alternative. One would have been to provide all buildings in the town (residences, business establishments and community buildings) with photovoltaic solar panels and allow daytime surplus electricity to be fed into batteries, and the whole town provided electricity as "stand-alone mini-grid". This was possibly a less costly option. The diesel generator would have remained as a back-up.

If the Windorah case is used as an excuse to permanently rule out solar power in the outback, this would be the wrong decision. There are numerous remote communities and small towns scattered in isolated parts of the nation that would benefit through reduced expenditure on diesel, and will, due to the less diesel used, make a small contribution to reducing greenhouse gases.

6.

The Sunshine Coast Goes Solar in a Carbon Off-Set

TOR HUNDLOE AND KEELEY HARTZER

Queensland deserves its title as "the Sunshine State". North of Brisbane, roughly the same travelling time as it is from Brisbane to the Gold Coast (about one hour), is what is formally called the Sunshine Coast. The former is a city of approximately 600,000 residents, the latter is what in Queensland is called a Regional Council area. It has a population of about half the Gold Coast.

The Sunshine Coast has in the order of 60 per cent of the population of the state of Tasmania. The Tasmanian capital, Hobart, has about 70 per cent of the Sunshine Coast's population, and this Queensland local authority has more than twice the population of Darwin. On the basis of population, the Sunshine Coast, as a city, is the ranked number nine in Australian. These facts are presented to illustrate that the Sunshine Coast is no small local authority with its residents having little impact on Australia, including the emissions of greenhouse gases.

The Sunshine Coast made history in 2017. It is the first city-sized local authority in Australia to run the totality of the local government's operations on solar electricity. The council's vehicles are excluded. In undertaking this project, the matter of the availability of land for a medium-sized solar farm was crucial. Obviously, the Sunshine Coast is no outback town surrounded by very low value arid land. Coastal land tends to have high economic value, and this could very easily rule out a solar farm of any size. If the land that was eventually chosen for the solar farm had have been on the Gold Coast, it is likely to have been engineered into canal estates for millionaires to purchase. But then the Sunshine Coast has not become a replica of its southern neighbour.

The local governments elected by Sunshine Coast residents have over a long period of time taken the view that the area will remain much more natural than its Gold Coast rival. There are limits on building heights; construction on the in-tact frontal dunes is forbidden; and there are very few canal estates eating into mangrove ecosystems. This has resulted in a physical environment not that different from what the Gold Coast's was in the 1960s before the "developers" came and were encouraged to transform the city. This is explained in detail in the book *The Gold Coast Transformed*.

The Sunshine Coast comprises golden beaches, frontal dunes in the areas where wise governments intervened before the developers had their way, coastal flood plains along the rivers that wind their way from the hinterland to the ocean, cleared farming land with a variety of uses (but mainly sugar cane growing), and finally the mountainous rainforests to the west.

From the late 19th century on, the Sunshine Coast flood plains were cleared to grow sugar cane. The history of sugar production in Australia is one where farms were located in reasonably proximity to a sugar mill. Enough sugar farmers in an area and a mill was built. Obviously, this kept the cost of transporting the cane to a minimum. The Moreton Sugar Mill, in the centre of the small Sunshine Coast town of Nambour, opened in 1897. The last cane train to deliver cut cane to the mill rolled into the town on 3 December 2003. From that date on, the sugar cane farmers who remained in the Sunshine Coast district were forced to transport their cane a distance of 160 km to the Maryborough mill. The added cost affected the financial viability of many farmers. The 2004 season resulted in numerous bare-land farms. What was to become of the land?

The future use of this former sugar cane land was not just an economic and environmental issue, it was political in the sense that the local community was interested, and the regional shire council had to attempt to reconcile conflicting land-use objectives. In 2009, the Sunshine Coast Regional Council produced its "Canelands Discussion Paper". A solar farm was not on the agenda. However, the idea was jellying at the time. Also, in 2009 the Sunshine Coast Regional Council commissioned a study called "Regional Energy Opportunities".

The local government folk were seeking forward-looking strategies that went beyond traditional land uses. In mid-2010, the Sunshine Coast Regional Council adopted a "Climate Change and Peak Oil Strategy". This was a far more radical policy initiative than produced at higher levels of government in Australia. The notion of peak oil was not then and still is not on most government agendas in Australia. History should record this as a revolutionary project at local government level in Australia. At the end of 2010, the Council adopted its "Energy Transition Plan" and history was about to be made. The plan allowed renewable energy production as a complement to farming on rural land. Protecting farming land in Australia is second to the belief in motherhood.

The Sunshine Regional Council's plan opened up the question, would good quality agricultural land be made available for conversion to a solar farm? Governments, including the Sunshine Coast Regional Council, have been keen to dodge the controversy that arose some years back when prime food-producing land in the US was converting to growing grains for bio-fuel production.

Here we leave temporarily the dilemma faced on the Sunshine Coast. The question of determining on a national scale if land was suitable for either solar or wind farms was addressed in 2012 by the Australian Energy Market Operator. It commissioned the consulting firm Roam Consulting to undertake the task (see Roam Consulting, 2012). The results of the study were in general practical and sensible. For example, grazing land, both natural and improved pastures, was deemed suitable for installing wind farms due to their very tiny footprint; natural grazing land, of which Australia has an enormous amount, was deemed suitable for solar farms; forestry areas were ruled out for obvious reasons; cropping and horticulture land was not entirely excluded, but all land used intensively was, including that used for intensive horticulture. Under this assessment, existing sugar cane farms were not to give way to solar farms. Retired sugar cane land, being no longer productive in its original use, was not a category considered. The Sunshine Coast Regional Council could make its own determination.

One vacant sugar cane farm was to become the site for the country's first local-authority developed solar farm, and when it started operating in mid-2017 the fifth largest solar farm in Australia. It is named Valdora. The mayor, Mark Jamieson, remarked that many other regional councils were taking notice. Valdora is a 49-ha block of land situated between the Maroochy River and the Yandina-Coolum Road. In the order of 20 ha is covered with 48,000 photovoltaic solar panels. The panels are raised above the flood level as this is flood plain country. The panels have the capacity to provide 15 MW of electricity. This is enough electricity to power all the Sunshine Coast Regional Council's administration buildings, aquatic centres (swimming pools), community venues, sporting venues, holiday parks, libraries and art galleries. The amount of electricity is equivalent to that required for 5,000 households. The electricity is fed into the grid, not directed to the council facilities. There is a grid network sub-station on the border of the solar farm. Close proximity to the grid is a significant economic benefit.

It could be asked why did not the Council simply install photovoltaic solar panels on its buildings and service centres? At the time that the Valdora project was being planned there were already 30,000 rooftop solar arrays on residences and small business premises on the Sunshine Coast. The number has increased substantially since then. The Council's problem was that its roof space was limited. For example, its numerous public swimming pools and aquatic centres, which are the main users of electricity, have virtually no roof space on which to install solar panels. A solar farm was the answer.

There was some public opposition to the development of the solar farm including legal challenges, however the local authority won these. Aesthetics and glare were the source of the challenges. Residents in distant hillslopes do have a partial view of the site, but distance and vegetation screening overcame the problem.

The capital cost is reported to have been $50.4 million. The net benefit savings in electricity bills for the Council plus money earned from the excess electricity sold into the grid has been estimated at $22.1 million over 30 years, based on present electricity costs. The Valdora solar farm is expected to save over 20,000 tonnes of carbon dioxide annually. That is in the order of 40,000 tonnes of coal not burned, and consequently is a significant reduction in greenhouse gases compared to the situation before the solar farm was built. The off-sets are, therefore, two-fold: reduced electricity bills and reduced greenhouse gas emissions. Whether or not Valdora has a demonstration effect with other local authorities following suit only time will tell. Not all, or even many, will have the opportunity to use vacant flat land close to grid sub-station.

If we made assumptions about the damage avoided by reducing emissions, we could put an economic value, over-and-above any money earned by the Council from sales of excess electricity, on the solar farm. For the sake of illustration, if we assume the carbon tax that was in place in Australia for a short period (set at $23 per tonne of carbon) is a reasonable estimate of the damage per tonne of carbon emissions, the result is that just under one-half a million dollars in damage is avoided each year into perpetuity (if the solar farm is maintained indefinitely). We could use a much higher carbon price. For example, in 2006 Nicholas Stern suggested a range of US$25 to US$85 per tonne. Based on the high estimate, the value would be US$1.7 million annually.

All in all, the Valdora solar farm is impressive. It is comparatively small compared to the ones that are being constructed as we write. And to "put the icing on the cake", the Sunshine Coast Regional Council staff are exploring running sheep on the farm. The Australian model for this (there are overseas ones) is the University of Queensland's very small solar farm at Gatton (see the cover).

SECTION III

Global Perspectives and Good Ideas

7.

What Can We Learn from Other Countries?

TOR HUNDLOE

As climate change is a global problem, in the long run (hopefully short that it be) we are destined to bring to bear a global perspective on solving it. At present, notwithstanding the Paris Accord (the global plan to limit global warming to be below 2 degrees celsius), each nation is following its own agenda in seeking to meet that international agreement. Australia's focus over the past 10 years has been on energy and specifically electricity. As noted throughout this book we have struggled with this as public policy, but as citizens and increasingly business people we have taken matters into our own hands and become a world leader in household solar roof top panels. However, there is no reason why we should not look beyond our borders in search for more ideas, particularly at utility-scale electricity generation.

It is not only the European and north American experience that we can draw on. We will figuratively visit the vast Sahara

Desert stretching across northern Africa, from Morocco to Egypt. Virtually anywhere in this desert vast solar farms would not interfere with people or their pursuits. Farming and human occupation is not feasible, life is found only at the occasional small oasis with a tiny cluster of date palms. We will use this example to show the enormous potential that Australia has if we were to utilise our deserts for solar electricity generation.

We will come to discuss the concept of Australia exporting solar electricity, not a far-fetched idea, and to pay due regard to free trade policies, we must also consider Australia importing electricity. The latter was close to happening. This very interesting idea, which for reasons not made public, has been relegated to the "back burner" after much publicity announcing it not that many years ago, in 2010. The idea was to import hydro-electricity from PNG, which is closer to Australia than Tasmania is to the mainland. PNG has world-class hydro-electricity potential. It could be, with its very high rainfall and resulting fast flowing rivers and small rural population, a hydro-electricity "super power", the Norway of Oceania.

In a future scenario, we could be importing hydro-electricity from PNG while exporting solar-generated electricity to Indonesia. The economists' law of comparative advantage lurks. Exporting to Indonesia was originally floated many years ago. It has resurfaced recently with headlines like the following produced by Professor Andrew Campbell in referring to Australia's outback and desolate north: "The north's future is electrifying: powering Asia with renewables". Another notable expert, Ariel Liebman from Monash University, is also worth quoting: "Australia's energy future lies across the Timor Sea (with an) Indonesian-Australian renewable energy Super Grid". A very large solar farm could be built in the Pilbara–Kimberly area of Western Australia and electricity sent via sub-sea, high-voltage direct cable transmission the 2,000 km to Java. This idea is not necessarily farfetched. The magazine *RenewEconomy* on 15 October 2015 ran the headline "Solar fuels could be Australia's biggest energy export".

Before exploring the concept of international trade in electricity let us step back and highlight a few interesting facts that put Australia's electricity consumption into perspective. Where do we sit in a league table?

Putting electricity consumption around the world on a per household, or per person, basis gives rise to unexpected, somewhat puzzling results, particularly at the high-consumption end. The average United States and Canadian households use nearly 12,000 kWh/year (around 4,500 kWh/per annum/per capita). On the other hand, households in France and Japan use about one-half the North American amount. German households sit not far above the world average. Australia's annual household consumption is in the order of 6,000 kWh. We use half the amount of the Americans. Expect to find slightly different estimates if you search multiple sources. We have rounded the numbers and used various sources to "average out" the estimates.

At the bottom of the world rankings on electricity availability and use are many sub-Saharan countries. One country with a large and growing population is Nigeria. Its annual household consumption of electricity is in the order of 570 kWh. For perspective, that of India is about 900 kWh, and China's is approaching 1,400 kWh. Virtually every household in China (with an average population of three persons) has electricity. In Nigeria, the average household is five persons and under half the households have electricity.

Australians delight in comparing themselves to other nationalities. Five countries, other than Australia, have come to dominate the solar and wind-power revolution, Germany, Spain, Portugal, Denmark and the USA. By selecting these five we don't mean to downplay the very significant achievements and the enthusiasm the Chinese have brought to the manufacture of solar panels. And we cannot omit from discussion India. It is already the most heavily populated country in the world, and in contrast to its near equal in human numbers today, China, its population will continue to expand while China's will fall. An expanding population is going to prove a major problem for India, not only in eliminating electricity poverty. Lack of electricity for the hundreds of millions of poor is one of the most basic social and economic problems in India.

There is little need to describe the German enthusiasm for renewable electricity. We have already drawn attention to the German government's "first-mover" push in giving a helping hand to renewables, stretching back to the early 1990s. To appreciate the seriousness of the German government in meeting the renewable challenge one only needs to view the extensive solar and wind installations the Germans have on the ground. In this case, seeing is believing. Political commitment (involving feed-in tariffs and subsidies) has been fundamental to the growth of renewable electricity.

In 2010, a report prepared in co-operation between the German Federal Ministry of Economics and Technology and the Federal Ministry for the Environment, Nature Conservation and Nuclear Safety put it thus: "Securing a reliable, economically viable and environmentally sound energy supply is one of the great challenges of the 21st century". While this statement is not radical in its self, what grabs attention are the government departments involved. Economic and environmental matters are viewed as one. This is a prerequisite for success.

Electricity based on renewable sources is high on the agenda of Denmark, Spain and Portugal. Danish windmills are as well-known as Hans Christian Anderson's Little Mermaid. More so than cheese, pork and pastries, wind power defines modern Denmark. In southern Europe, sunny Portugal and Spain make the international news with their roll-out of solar energy. Spain has been very successful in its export of solar technologies. Its products and expertise are evident in Australia where Spanish firms are major players. This fact begs the question, why as a scientific leader in solar technology do we in Australia end up importing both technology and operational-cum-management expertise from Spain?

Spain's neighbour Portugal has, amongst an array of renewable energy installations, a small (11 MW capacity) photovoltaic solar farm, covering about 150 acres with the panels high enough to allow grazing below them. Obviously, this is an attempt to address the issue of taking productive land out of agricultural production. We mention this Portuguese project to make a key point: the siting of large solar farms cannot be allowed to sterilise high-quality productive agricultural land, particularly given farming is set to become much more important and profitable, as globally limited land and water resources are being asked to feed an increasing human population, an increase of over two billion in the next 30 years. Some Australian solar farms allow sheep grazing under and around the panels.

It is relatively easy for northern Europe to be environmentally friendly in the use of electricity. For example, when Denmark is not producing sufficient electricity from its windmills, it can turn to hydro-electricity from its Scandinavian neighbours, Norway and Sweden. If Denmark takes all its imported electricity from Norway, it can claim to be a totally green electricity consumer. Norway's electricity comes from hydro-electric plants. The Europeans are proving that seamless integration of intermittent electricity sources with the conventional sources is feasible. This matter remains a struggle in Australia.

Then there is the United States. There is a tendency to think of it as a solar energy laggard, notwithstanding the efforts of Al Gore to awaken its citizens, and the rest of the world, to the perils of climate change. With refusals by US federal governments to play ball in international greenhouse gas reduction policies, and powerful fossil-fuel lobbyists dictating policies, one is surprised to learn of the progressive history of solar and wind power in the United States.

As with many of the advanced technologies of the present era, we can thank the US industrial-military complex for the development of solar energy technology. In various industrial research fields, enormous government largesse allowed the US military establishment to undertake the blue-sky thinking and laboratory work that, when successful and eventually passed on to commercial hands, proved very profitable. Think the internet. In the case of solar power, we note the very early US spacecraft, in particular satellites, were equipped with solar panels. This was in the late 1950s as the US establishment reacted to the embarrassment that came from knowing the nation's citizens went outside of a night seeking a glimpse of the Soviet Union's Sputnik 1. At that point, in October 1957 the Soviet Union had won the space race.

We have not the space to tell the story of government-funded research and commercial uptake of renewable electricity in the US. However, we can note that in the early 1970s and again in the late 1970s, the dramatic oil price increases (orchestrated by the Arab nations in response to US support for Israel) forced the US government to become serious about energy security. There was also a keen interest in "the end of oil" thesis.

The time was ripe for a serious consideration of renewable energy during President Carter's term in office. The availability and cost of petrol and diesel ("gas" in US terminology) focussed the minds of the average US citizen. Carter and the US Congress did not neglect solar and wind-generated electricity. Today, sun-blessed US States are amongst the world leaders in renewable electricity generation. This is possible where state governments can run their own agenda regardless of the policies made in Washington. Note in passing that this is also the situation in Australia. Our State and Territory governments do not have wait for leadership at the national level; however, the fact that we have the interconnected east coast grid, and the Commonwealth government's legislated renewable energy targets, gives the Commonwealth a key role.

In the 1980s solar power plants started to appear in the Mojave Desert in Nevada. Here is some of the best insolation in the US. Both solar thermal and photovoltaic plants were built. The fundamental point is that desert locations, where the opportunity cost in terms of taking land out of competing uses is insignificant, were chosen for solar farms.

There was, and remains, one issue to resolve if solar thermal plants are located in desert areas—the lack of water for cooling. These solar farms gather solar radiation in panels and direct it to a concentrator/absorber. The result is a very high temperature fluid or molten salt that is used to produce steam to drive a turbine (to turn a generator) to produce electricity. This is no different to coal-fired or uranium power stations. In all these cases cooling is necessary. Water is not what we expect to find in deserts. The technology for "dry cooling" electricity plants, although expensive, exists. Photovoltaic systems do not have this problem as the electricity is produced directly in the panels.

To continue with our desert theme, we venture to the Sahara Desert. How many headlines like the following have you read: "Could the desert power the world?" This one is from the *Guardian*, 12 December 2011. The story is told of a German physicist, Gerhard Knies, who calculated—back of an envelope style—that in only six hours the world's deserts receive more energy from the sun than the word's human population uses in one year. Based on his estimate, an area the size of Wales (or 0.3 per cent of the sunlight falling on the Sahara Desert and the Middle Est.) could provide electric power for the whole of Europe. Several organisations, including the IPPC and WWF International have noted the potential of producing massive amounts of solar-based electricity in deserts.

We let the overseas experience suggest possibilities for Australia. Australia's desert solar irradiation is close to that of the Sahara Desert. How much electricity would be produced if parts of the Australian deserts were to become efficient, concentrated solar farms? First another question.

How much of the planet's land would need to be covered by solar panels to supply the world's population with electricity? Experts suggest that it would only take three per cent using concentrated solar panels. Knies, who we mentioned before, had a grand plan for massive solar farms in the Sahara (particularly in Morocco) to transmit electricity to Europe.

The idea failed to attract the necessary funding, in part due to perceived political instability in northern Africa. The failure of the Knies' scheme led the Moroccans to go it alone. In early 2016, a 160 MW capacity concentrated solar power facility started to produce electricity for domestic use in Morocco. This plant is the first of three planned for the desert outside of the town of Ouarzazate. The proposal is that 6,000 acres are to be covered by panels to produce both photovoltaic and concentrated thermal solar electricity. Rated at a total of 500 MW capacity, the project, if and when completed, would provide enough electricity to service a Moroccan city of two million inhabitants.

The above has been an extremely brief sketch of major renewable electricity initiatives in some of the key industrialised countries. The story is dramatically different once we leave those countries. The contrast is most stark if we venture into sub-Sahara Africa. Let us hear from the authors of the "Africa Progress Report 2015" (page 34):

> Today, in the first quarter of the 21st century, most Africans have yet to experience the benefits of modern energy, including the light bulb. Viewed from the world's most affluent countries, it is easy to lose sight of the role that energy has played in development. Affordable and reliable electricity underpins every aspect of social and economic life … it is no coincidence that power generation, access to energy, wealth and human development are closely associated.

What do the poor of the world do for lighting, cooking and operating any rudimentary machinery that they might have? Kerosene is used for a wide range of household purposes. Even kerosene is far too expensive for the very poor, and cooking is done on wood-burning stoves. Where wood is scarce (as it is increasingly becoming in most of the poor world) there are other sources of biomass such as twigs and dried leaves picked from the ground and, if the nearby land is grazed, there will be dung. These sources of energy are burned in very low-efficiency stoves, many placed inside chimney-less dwellings.

It is estimated by the World Health Organization that in the order of 3 billion people (over 40 per cent of the global population) cook their food on the most basic biomass-fuelled stoves. They are commonly called "three-stone" stoves because they comprise nothing more than this number of stones arranged vertically on which a pot of stewing food sits, the fire underneath filling the nearby air with fine particulate pollution, some of it extremely dangerous to humans if lodged in the lungs.

The marginally better-off can afford kerosene cookers. Methane results from inefficient combustion of kerosene and this contributes to global warming. The black smoke that is ever present with the use of kerosene is "soot". It is more accurately described as "black carbon". The positive side of biomass-fuelled cooking fires is that they produce less black carbon than burning kerosene. Half of deaths of children under five years of age are a result of particulate matter (soot) inhaled. When the World Health Organization looks to the future, there is no relief as the total number of people relying on these health-destroying fuels is likely to remain unchanged in 2030.The renewable electricity revolution which we are living through is not predicted to go beyond the shores of the planet's rich or soon to be rich, in the latter case the Chinese.

While it is not the focus of our book to explore inequality and economic under-development in the poor world, it is important to recognize that inequality is not just in income and food but in access to electricity. The latter exacerbates the existing social divisions within the poor countries. There is a stark difference between Third World slum dwellers and rural populations compared to their fellow wealthy urban dwellers with their electric appliances as sophisticated as those owned by a middle-class Australian household.

At present electricity provides 17 per cent of the world's final energy consumption. The Paris-based International Energy Agency (IEA) predicts that by 2050 global electricity demand will have increased to be 23 per cent of total energy demand. Image a world without energy, especially electricity. The result, poverty.

8.

Importing Renewable Electricity

KEELEY HARTZER AND TOR HUNDLOE

> This project would mean our vision for a stronger, greener Queensland could take a giant leap forward. It would be the biggest shot in the arm for regional Australia since the Snowy River scheme … This project would provide PNG with a reliable source of power for villages and rural communities and transform the economic development prospects of western Papua New Guinea … this is a first step towards making Queensland the renewable energy star of Australia … It means Queensland can power Australia's economy using one of the greenest forms of energy on earth.
>
> Anna Bligh, Previous Premier of Queensland
> (15/9/2010, media statement)

The quote above relates to one of the most exciting renewable electricity projects in the South Pacific, if not the southern hemisphere. In this part of the world the idea of transmitting electricity between nations has received scant attention, so when someone as influential as a Premier makes a statement like the one reported above, one takes notice.

In this unique case, we have two sovereign governments agreeing to export/import electricity on the basis of significant mutual benefits. The project is known as the Purari River Hydro Electric Project. The Purari River flows from the PNG highlands (with its catchment reaching to near Mt. Hagen), then south into the Coral Sea. Its catchment is one of the highest rainfall areas in PNG. The rainfall is consistent and at the main village in the region, Wabo, it averages approximately eight metres per year. No small amount. The catchment is very sparsely populated which means very little dispossession of local villagers if flooding by a large hydro-electric dam is the result. The economic returns from the project would allow significant compensation to anyone who has to move, and in economic terms they should be much better off. Of course, displacement has other effects, particularly in a traditional tribal society where attachment to land is of great cultural significance.

Ultimately, the three legs of the sustainability stool come into play with projects like this: the social, the environmental and the economic. In tribal societies each of these matters has implications and consequences very much different to those in the industrialised societies. In the Purari River case, the "triple bottom line" matters are yet to be studied and resolved; but on the positive side what we can report is that a series of studies over the past 40 years (some undertaken by the Snowy

Mountains Engineering Corporation) have identified the river as suitable for a hydro-electric dam. One tick out of three.

On 14 September 2010, the then Queensland Premier, Anna Bligh, and PNG Minister for State Assisting the Prime Minister on Constitutional Matters, Moss Maladina, signed a "Memorandum of Cooperation" (with PNG Energy Developments Ltd and Origin Energy Limited as the partners). This was to be a 50:50 joint venture between the two companies.

The project required a major dam be built near the village of Wabo, which is 198 kilometres upstream. Given very limited demand for electricity in this part of PNG, most of it would be transmitted to the PNG south coast, then undersea (using the same technology used in the Bass Strait undersea link) to the Australian mainland where conventional poles and wires would take the electricity into Bamaga, on to Weipa and join the east coast grid at Townsville. As dispatchable (24/7) hydro-electricity, it would be a significant contributor to lessening the disruption caused by intermittent solar and wind power in Australia.

The project was costed at $5 billion and have a 2,500 MW capacity. To put this in perspective, consider this newspaper report on the front page of the *Australian* 3 July 2017: "New analysis … reveals it would cost $2.2 billion to build a 1,000 MW ultra-supercritical coal power plant". This so called "highly-efficient, low-emission" coal-fired power plant is proposed for north Queensland. On this basis, a 2,500 MW coal-fired plant would cost $5.5 billion. Taking into account the low inflation rate that has pertained in recent years, the

PNG hydro-electric proposal is on par or wins on financial grounds: $5 billion versus $5.5 billion. As its fuel (flowing water) is free and no greenhouse gases are admitted during operation its benefits far outweigh its costs.

Another perspective is to compare the cost of this hydro-electricity plant and the amount of aid Australia provides to PNG. Over the past 10 years this has been approximately $5 billion. In making this comparison this is not to suggest the hydro-electric scheme is or should be part of our aid program—the hydro-electric scheme is a corporate sector proposal with the potential to earn normal profits.

This is not the end of what looked likely be a story with a happy ending. In March 2014, Origin Energy put the proposal on the "back burner", citing the then low price of electricity and the fact that the project would not be allowed to be participate in Australia's renewable energy target, due to the fact the law governing this was written so that only electricity generated in Australia was entitled to be included. This need not be the final word on the project. The Australian parliament has only to amend the law for Origin Energy to reconsider the proposal—or for the price of electricity to increase! We checked with Origin Energy Limited in late 2017 and were told that the project was not a priority as "solar-based electricity had become the priority".

The excitement and enthusiasm generated when the proposal was first mooted is worth revisiting. Rowan Callick, the Asia-Pacific Editor of the *Australian* wrote on 17 September 2010:

> If the new project succeeds, this will at last provide the long-sought steel pin linking the neighbouring countries in mutual benefit that has been lacking since PNG gained independence from Australia on September 16th, 1975—35 years ago.

When researching this story, a newspaper article reported that the Purari River was the pick-up point for shipments of marijuana and the drop-off point for military weapons and explosives. The story suggested that submarines were used as carriers. Drugs and guns versus electricity!

News reports suggest that China is taking a more serious interest in financing projects in PNG than Australia is. Make of this what you will. We asked the previous Commonwealth environment and energy minister, Josh Frydenberg, if he had a view on the Purari River hydro-electricity project. He had not heard of it.

9.

Exporting Solar Electricity

TOR HUNDLOE

If Australia is able to important electricity, we should be able to export it. Exporting would not to be to our nearest neighbour, PNG. As discussed in the previous chapter, it has the resources to produce an immense amount of hydro-electricity. We will need to look north-west from the top of Western Australia to Indonesia. The electricity that we could produce for export would be generated by very large solar farms in the Western Australia.

Covering deserts with solar panels comes at little or no opportunity cost, in other words no profitable land-use, such as agriculture, has to give way to the solar electricity industry. We should note, notwithstanding our single focus on solar power, that the same argument applies to off-shore wind farms. While the oceans are productive sources of seafood and have to be open to shipping, the footprint of a wind turbine is very small and little, if anything, productive is lost. Wind farms on on-shore with their tiny footprints are compatible with most agricultural pursuits. The third leg of our renewable troika, pumped hydro-electricity, can be developed in environments where there are no existing productive or otherwise valuable land uses.

There are 10 good-sized deserts in Australia, and a large part of the rest of the country is semi-arid. Semi-arid land has value in running cattle and sheep, but on a per hectare basis it comes at minimal opportunity cost if it can be put to other worthwhile uses. Estimates of the extent of arid and semi-arid land differ, but we can work with 70 per cent of this extremely large nation as arid plus semi-arid. To be more precise, one-fifth accounts for the 10 large deserts, and one-third if all deserts are included. There is another estimate which is that between 40 and 50 per cent comprises sand dunes (flat land is needed for solar farms). Even massive solar farms will hardly make a dint in the available outback land.

To be fair to our pastoralists we must pay heed to the extraordinary ability of Australians to graze beef cattle and sheep on some of the most desolate country on earth, where cattle and sheep are run on hectares per individual animal. This means that this land has some economic value, little may it be. We anticipate that the he value of the electricity produced per hectare will be considerable more than the value of wool or beef per hectare. Of course, this is subject to analysis. Consider the cost of transport. Cattle, sheep and wool have to be brought to market, that means a coastal city, and/or a port if exported as wool and much beef is. There is considerable cost involved when transported from the far-flung outback. The so-called "beef roads" were built to reduce the costs to the graziers. The cost of transmitting electricity from the middle of Australia to the major grids is an important part of the equation. New, state-of-the-art transmission lines will need to be built.

If we contemplate exporting electricity from the outback to, say, Indonesia (or Timor Leste), the poles and wires have to extend to a northern coastal destination before joining a sub-sea cable. Constructing the poles and wires is an expensive undertaking. Yet, if the solar farm or farms where near the Western Australian coast this would be but a minor part of the transmission cost.

The story, as it is today, about the possibilities of selling electricity into Indonesia is not complete without paying due regard to David Mills. It was his idea. He is one of three eminent Australian solar researchers. It is probably fair comment to suggest that their efforts, and results, have not resulted in governments or investors making the most of these scientists' research. There was the pioneering research done by Roger Morse in the 1960s on solar hot water systems. He was with the forerunner of CSIRO. More recently, until he left Australia in 2007, there was the excellent research by David Mills. Mills was at the University of Sydney for more than 30 years before he gave up searching for the necessary funding needed to progress both thermal and photovoltaic solar electricity. His early work was on advancing solar water-heating technology from which he moved on to the other applications of solar technology. From the 1970s until well into the 1990s, Australia was leading the world in research on both thermal and photovoltaic forms of solar energy.

When countries such as Germany, Spain, Japan and Korea started to pour considerable public money into solar photovoltaics, Australian governments did not keep pace. David Mills has entrepreneurial spirit and looked to a future when Australia would have power lines and under-water cables running from its north into Indonesia, carrying the electricity we generated in the outback deserts. The idea of selling electricity into Indonesia gets some airplay today as we have noted. Too late for David Mills who has sought greener (dollar) research pastures overseas.

Sydney did not have one but two eminent scientists researching and making world-class breakthroughs in solar electricity. The other chap is Professor Martin Green of the University of New South Wales. He finds time to be a director of the Australian National Energy Agency (ARENA). Of many scientific advancements, Green's dramatic improvement in the efficiency of silicon solar panels stands out. For a reader interested in a well written popular book on solar energy, Martin Green's *Power to the People* is highly recommended. The title comes from John Lennon's famous song of that name, recorded in 1971.

SECTION IV

The Conclusion

10.

The Revolution Continues

TOR HUNDLOE AND KEELEY HARTZER

At the beginning of this book we were confident enough to declare that here in Australia we are witness to the early days of a revolution which will to take us from reliance on fossil fuels to generate electricity to a future where we utilise our abundant sunshine and wind, complemented with pumped-stored hydro (and possibly ocean and geothermal sources) to provide the electricity we use in our homes, commercial buildings and industries.

The revolution is evident if in slow descent flying into the city of Brisbane you casually glance through the aircraft window to the roof tops you are skimming over. You will be struck by the metallic blue or black shimmers on many roofs. What you are seeing are photovoltaic solar panels gathering sunlight, converting it into electricity, and were more is generated than needed to power the electric devices in the house this excess is sold to the electricity grid that has its poles and wires poking into every suburban street. In some Brisbane suburbs approximately, 50 per cent of houses have solar panels on their roofs. Brisbane is the solar capital of the world on a per capita basis.

Not only is it in Brisbane but our other major cities, with Adelaide going-neck-to-neck with Brisbane, and towns such as centre-of-Australia Alice Springs that we find roofs adorned with the metallic blue and black devices that capture the sunlight and seemingly magically turn it into the electricity for the house's inhabitants. Australia is the world leader in roof top solar installations on a per capita basis, with Belgium running a poor second at around seven per cent of households compared to nearing 20 per cent, and growing, in Australia.

Turning our focus on solar farms, they have well and truly won the economic race. As of writing in mid-2018, solar-generated electricity can be purchased from these farms at less than $50 per MWh, compared to the cost of coal-generated electricity at $65 per MWh and gas-generated at $90 per MWh. The price of solar electricity will continue to fall.

And it is not only sunlight weaving its magic that is at the forefront of the electricity-generation revolution. Drive through the coastal farmlands of Victoria, South Australia, the north-west of Tasmania, south-west of Western Australia and (soon-to-be) south-east Queensland (that is a far stretch of Australia) and come to view the tall, elegant turbines that form the modern wind farm. Appreciate, as Australian bush folk have done for eons, the ease by which wind produces energy, whether it be to suck up artesian water to feed stock or in its modern form drive the electric shears in our shearing sheds, the milking machines on our dairy farms, and help power our large industries and our individual households. Wind-generated electricity runs second to solar at lower than $55 per MWh. It will also continue in a downward price trend.

If we were to select a sub-title for our book there are various ones that we could have used to describe the revolution. Some authors in selecting a title for their particular revolution have a liking for "the end of"—such as "the end of the stone age" or "the end of civilisation". Other writers, barracking for the other team, opt for "the beginning of"—"the beginning of the agricultural revolution". Then there are those who do not accept that their work is done but rather make a "call to revolution"—"workers of the world unite".

We could use each and all of these forms of a sub-titles. There is no doubt that "the end of fossil fuels" for electricity generation is inevitable. It is approaching quite fast in the industrialised world. However, there is the rest of the world to consider—many countries and vast numbers of poor people, some very poor, to consider. We cannot be confident that in the poor countries we will see the end of carbon-based energy sources for a considerable time yet. The under investment in the new technologies, such as solar and wind farms or hydro-electric schemes, due to the lack of profitable opportunities and the existence of sovereign risk are locking most poor countries into their old, existing technologies. This means that in poor countries where coal is presently used it will continue to be burned in utility-scale power stations. And the poorest of the poor will remain unconnected to any form of electricity and will continue to burn (expensive) kerosene and search for the increasingly scarce branches, twigs and leaves to fire their three-stone stoves. If you are the poorest of the poor, little changes.

Yet, in due course we are optimistic that the time will come for the end of fossil fuels even in the poorest parts of the world. Many poor countries, if not individually but in co-operation with neighbours, have abundant renewable resources to utilise. For example, massive hydro-electricity schemes could be built in sub-Sahara Africa. One need do no more than consult a map of this region and trace through the length of some of the planet's mightiest rivers and waterfalls. Because they run through numerous countries, co-operation will be essential. Large hydro-electric dams come at some environmental and social cost. But that is par for the course, unavoidable trade-offs if the poor are not to be denied electricity and a lifestyle approaching that of ours.

Enormous solar farms could be constructed in the desert country of sun-blessed areas of the globe. Already Morocco is proving that this is feasible. It is a serious proposition for Australia, not only for domestic use of electricity but for export. Understandably the cost-benefit analysis has to be done before we will know for certain whether this is feasible or not.

Many poor parts of the world will find themselves using a combination of renewable electricity-generating sources—solar, wind and small-scale hydro. The post fossil-fuel world is not going to revert to dismal and dark societies without electricity—the replacement sources for fossil-fuel electricity exist. There is no need to wish for their invention.

So far so good for a renewable electricity future.

But here we need to mention a topic that is not a subject of this book, but a fundamental project in the transformation of human societies from fossil fuels, and that is the electrification of transport. Powering our homes, commercial buildings and industries with renewable electricity will be, when it is complete, a revolution; however, it will only go so far in reducing global warming and our reliance on non-renewable energy sources.

We drive to work, to the shops, the sports fields and various other places in petrol or diesel-powered cars. Our food, white goods, clothing and all sorts of products are moved around this vast nation in trucks fuelled by fossil fuels. We are some years away from the electrification of transport. We have electric trains, trams and buses and a few cars and electric push bikes but they draw their electricity in the main from a major grid. At present most of the electricity they use is derived from fossil-fuels.

Not only are we waiting for the mass production of electric vehicles and contemplating the possibility of hydrogen-fuelled cars and trucks, but we wait for the required infrastructure to be built so that we can take these vehicles out on the nation's highways and byways. Today petrol and diesel service stations dot our massive country, but virtually nowhere on the highways and byways can we plug in our electric vehicles for a battery charge.

Turning attention to a "beginning of" sub-title—the beginning of renewable energy—we do hope that the preceding chapters have convinced you that the renewable electricity generation revolution, based at the moment on roof-top solar panels, is well and truly under way. At the household level, you, dear reader, are at its vanguard.

What is being done in installing photovoltaic solar panels on household roofs is the crucial initial step in a comprehensive renewable energy future. As converts to solar power for our household electricity, we have achieved so much so soon that we are past the beginning of the beginning, if that makes sense. We are building a bottom up revolution, notwithstanding the vacillations and occasional regressions of our governments, particularly our Commonwealth governments, on policies to take us to a fossil-fuel free future

An issue that tends to be neglected in thinking about Australia's future electricity needs is population growth. The Australian population was estimated by the Australia Bureau of Statistics (ABS) to be 24,973,360 as of 13 July 2018. The ABS makes a mid-range prediction of 35.9 million in 2050, and 62.2 million to 70.1 million in 2101. The nation's current electricity consumption is approximately 235 Terawatt-hours (TWh). Only about 33 TWh are produced by renewables. The projections for electricity in Australia are 285 TWh in 2030, and 395 TWh by 2050. If all was to be from renewables that would require 12 times the present level of production; if only 50 per cent was to be from renewables the total increase from today would be six times.

The journey has a considerable way to go. We are on track.

References

ABC News, 14 December 2008.

ABC News, 30 May 2013.

African Progress Panel (2015) "Power People Planet: Seizing Africa's Energy and Climate Opportunities", Genova.

Australian, 17 September 2010.

Australian, 3 July 2017.

Australian, 3 July 2018.

Bernstein, P. (2008) *Economist on Wall Street*, John Wiley and Sons Ltd., New York.

Blyth, A. Media Statement, 15 September 2010.

Brisbane Times, 24 August 2016.

Byrnes, L., Brown, C., Foster, J., and Wagner, L. (2013) "Australian renewable energy policy: Barriers and Challenges", *Renewable Energy*, 60(1): 711–21.

Courier Mail, 11 February 2017.

Courier Mail, 7 July 2018.

Economist, 25 February 2017.

Finkel, A., Moses, K., Munro. C., Effeney, T., and O'Kane, M. (2017) "Independent Review into the Future Security of the National Electricity Market".

Goodall, C. (2016) *The Shift*, Profile Books, London.

Hundloe, T., McDougall, B. and Page, C. (2015) *The Gold Coast Transformed*, CSIRO Publishing, Collingwood.

Industry Commission (1991) "Energy Generation and Distribution", AGPS, Canberra.

New Scientist, 9 June 2018.

RenewEconomy, 15 October 2015.

Roam Consulting (2012), Brisbane.

Millar and Minchin (*The Age*, 31 January 2009), TBA.

Seifried, D. and Witzel, W. (2010) "Renewable Energy: The Facts", Earthscan, London.

Stern, N. (2006) *The Stern Report: The Economics of Climate Change*, Oxford University Press, Oxford.

Weekend Australian, 18–19 March 2017.

Wood, T., Blowers, D and Griffiths, K. (2018) *Down to the Wire*, The Grattan Institute, Melbourne.

Index

Printed in Australia
AUHW011500011020
334867AU00007B/11

9 781925 801453